A VERY PUBLIC OFFERING

A Rebel's Story of Business Excess, Success, and Reckoning

Stephan Paternot, Cofounder, theglobe.com
with Andrew Essex

JOHN WILEY & SONS, INC.

New York • Chichester • Weinheim • Brisbane • Singapore • Toronto

This publication is designed to provide accurate and authoritative information in regard to the subject matter covered. It is sold with the understanding that the publisher is not engaged in rendering professional services. If professional advice or other expert assistance is required, the services of a competent professional person should be sought.

Library of Congress Cataloging-in-Publication Data:

ISBN 0-471-00786-2

Printed in the United States of America.

10 9 8 7 6 5 4 3 2 1

To mom and dad, even from 10,000 miles away, somehow, you both brought out the best in me and helped me achieve my dreams . . . hopefully there'll be more. (Anders and Monica, thank you for keeping mom and dad . . . and me so happy.)

To Todd (Waddi), this journey could never have been made without you. Ready for the next one? ☺

To all my brothers, sisters, friends, and buddies at theglobe.com, many of whom were with me from my days in diapers through the ups and downs, highs and lows, good days and bad—and never left my side.
I will always be indebted to you.

Those who say it cannot be done should get out of the way of those who are doing it.

—*a wise fortune cookie*

Contents

PART 2

Acknowledgments

S pecial thanks to those I've met along the way who helped make all this possible. Brad Fuller, a chance meeting at 35,000 feet. Nick Stevens, Howie Sanders, Dan Mandel, Jeanne Glasser, Gray Coleman, Andrew Essex. Let's get ready to rumble!

PROLOGUE

a good day to go public

When I think about it now, I guess I should have been more concerned that we were going public on Friday the 13th. But sometimes you realize these things too late.

Not that it would have mattered: We didn't have much control over the timing.

> > >

I can still picture that morning in 1998. It was a cold, gray, November day, and the last leaves had fallen from the trees near my apartment just off Union Square. This was the Friday that my partner Todd and I were supposed to head over to the midtown offices of Bear Stearns, the investment bank that was taking us public. The night before we'd established an opening price of $9, and just in time because our S1 (the detailed SEC registration document) would go stale that following Monday. Friday was the last possible day to file before everything crapped out. Another delay would be a death sentence. If it didn't happen, we'd run out of money. In other words: game over. The sky was threatening to fall, and our mission was to keep it propped up.

I hadn't slept the night before, spending most of that time watching CNN and the White House announcement that five American aircraft carriers were heading for Iraq. War talk. Todd and I knew that a declaration of war, among other things, could really disrupt the market. I was up until about 3:00 or 4:00 in the morning, tossing and turning, thinking about all the things that could possibly go wrong. You don't get many chances to go public, and for a moment, it seemed like the stars were aligned against us.

At the time, I had a unique way of dealing with stress: TheraFlu, straight up, no chaser. Yet, even with an inordinate amount of over-the-counter medication in my system, the eve of the IPO was a long, restless night. At the time, my personal life was in as much tumultuous uncertainty as the market. That Friday evening, after the IPO, I was supposed to go out on a first date with a beautiful girl I'd recently met who was (and still is) the greatest thing that had happened to me in a long time. So I was doubly anxious. My biggest fear was, of course, that everything would go wrong. With possibilities of war, romance, and some serious banking all dancing in my head, I was scared sh*tless.

So, on Friday the 13th, I got out of bed at 7:00 A.M., showered, and dressed for a 9:30 meeting at Bear Stearns. My first thought was CNN. I switched it on and called Todd. "You watch the news?" The ships were on their way, but a declaration of war, at least for today, was now considered unlikely.

I couldn't eat breakfast due to the jitters and walked out of the apartment with an empty, quaking stomach.

> > >

Breakfast aside, what does one wear to an IPO? We'd thought for a moment about suits, but I deliberately remember thinking, No, I will not put on a suit. Todd and I always dressed casually. There's nothing greater than standing amidst all those bankers in suits while people wonder, Who are those two college boys in khakis and leather jackets? In retrospect, and in pictures, we were just two scruffy college kids in ratty sweaters.

By 9:00, the sky had turned blue, and it was a beautiful day. My nerves were calmed a little when I met Todd at the northeast corner of Union Square. We grabbed a cab straight up Park Avenue, through the underground passageway beneath Murray Hill, and up and around Grand Central, hurtling down the switchback. The cabby was speeding, but I wanted him to go faster. I remember we both had huge rings under our eyes. We looked like hell. Note to self: If you're going to look like crap, the day of your IPO is not the best day to do it.

We arrived at Bear Stearns at 9:15 with plenty of time to spare and passed quickly through the lobby. By then, we'd been there so many times they knew exactly who we were. Still, the interminable security check-in made us anxious as we headed into the elevator to meet the Bear Stearns people on the *13th floor*—another telling sign I missed at the time—where there were innumerable conference rooms, all marked alphabetically. We'd always met in conference rooms assigned boring, unsymbolic letters like H or M or L, and we wondered constantly what power plays occurred behind door A.

This time they ushered us into an even smaller and stuffier room than usual. Shortly thereafter, Ed Cespedes met us. Ed did M&A for Dancing Bear, the VC (venture capital) outfit formed by Michael Egan, the former Alamo Rent-A-Car president who'd ultimately sink $20 million into our company, theglobe.com. Ed was one of those guys who loved the job, loved the action of growing and creating companies. He'd been instrumental in setting this whole thing up, and we had a special bond with him. He'd turn out to be one of the few genuine good guys in this story.

Around 9:30, a few Stearns muckety-mucks swung by to make

sure we had the important tools: croissants, bagels, and gallons of coffee. I had a bagel with cream cheese, even though I still didn't have much of an appetite. (Whenever we'd gone to a banking deal at a law firm, they always had all this food lying around, so I'd end up stuffing my face. What I didn't know at the time was that I'd become lactose intolerant, which was why I continually suffered from big-time stomachaches.) As we sat around, pounding bagels with cream cheese and smiling vacantly at each other for what seemed an eternity, the stress started peaking at an exponential level, and the closer we got to show time, the more we felt that something was amiss, and the more my stomach hurt.

Then the bankers came in. I won't bother mentioning their names, since all the Bear Stearns people who worked with us are gone now—there's no one left for me to feel bitter toward anymore. Anyway, one of them came in and I couldn't contain myself anymore. "Are we going to *price?*" I blurted. "Is this thing going through, or what?"

"Yes, yes, yes," the banker said, casually.

"Oh, and by the way," he added with a grin, "word is it's going to open somewhere between $20 to $30 a share."

Here's what you should know. Forty-eight hours earlier, we'd struggled just to raise the price up to $8 a share. The best Bear Stearns had been able to do was raise our price by a dollar.

Naturally, Todd and I were flabbergasted by this new figure. I'd assumed we'd price at $9, and if the stock went up, it would happen later in the process. But that's not the way it goes down. In actuality, there's a buildup in the price as a stock goes onto the market. But somewhere between $20 to $30? That's 200 percent higher than we thought! This was absolutely insane. Despite the stomachache, both Todd and I were in giddy hysterics.

Meanwhile, we were still sitting there in that room, waiting, waiting, waiting. Waiting, waiting, waiting, waiting. Then, finally, at around 10:15, a few more bankers came to take us down to the second floor—the trading floor—a huge cavern with 400 traders, all eyeballs glued to their consoles and monitors, all screaming—like a scene out of *Wall Street*.

They led us through a narrow passageway that cut through the middle of the floor to the edge of the room, along this tiny walkway, like a prison catwalk above the inmates. At the end of the hall was a big corner office where Ace Greenberg sat.

Ace Greenberg is the chairman of Bear Stearns and a legend in the finance world. He's been there for some ungodly number of years, and everyone knows him. I remember thinking that if we were being handled by the chairman we were part of an omnipotent inner circle and would be well taken care of.

Ace is well known for doing card tricks. While we were sitting there, going insane from the anxiety, Ace did card tricks for us. Cards vanished out of his hands and then reappeared. He's so good at it, you actually wonder how the hell he did that.

About 10:35, another banker came in with an update. "Any minute now," he said. Ace's office was all glass windows. We could see the traders out in the middle of the floor; off in a pit, there's another pod of traders who will represent our deal. This particular banker kept shuffling back and forth between the two rooms like a gopher.

A few minutes later, he returned. He looked right at me and said, "By the way, the deal's not going to open at $20 to $30." He had this strange expression on his face, and I actually felt my heart beginning to break. Then he said, "It may hit between $50 and $60." I jumped out of my chair and said to no one in particular, "What the f*ck?"

Everyone burst out laughing. Even Ace.

At 10:50, the banker came back again. "All right, guys," he said, "let's go." We all walked down that little aisle, single file, like prisoners marching toward the gallows.

Down in the pit, I could see a few people eyeing us. Now remember, IPOs happen—at most—a few times a month at any given bank. So the pit people always make an effort to check and see who the lucky bastards are. Since we weren't in suits and we'd just been screaming, the people in the pit must have thought something really bizarre was going on. I'm sure someone said, "Who are those two kids? What the hell is this?"

Once past the pit, we were taken to a wall of computer screens set in a room that looked like an extension of the Millennium Falcon with all these monitors and triggers just ready to fire away. Three or four guys sat behind the screens, and there was one main guy behind them—the head pit boss for our trade.

This guy was too busy to talk to us. He was fiddling with papers, whispering numbers. I still had no idea what was going on. I checked out the screen, trying to understand something, but it was all completely unfamiliar. In other words, more waiting. Then I realized we were starting a countdown. The thing was going to happen at exactly the stroke of 11:00. All of a sudden, the main guy was counting, "Ten, nine, eight, seven. . . ." It was almost too much; Todd and I were in disbelief.

> > >

Do you want to know what an IPO feels like? Honestly? You feel like you're about to die. You're standing at heaven's gate, your whole life is flashing before you, and there's a judgment coming. We'd never done this before. We weren't bankers. We didn't know what it all meant. In my head, I'd worked out all these grossly exaggerated animated scenes, but then I'm standing there actually mumbling stupid things like a Warner Brothers cartoon character.

Then it hits. "Three, two, one. . . ."

Boom.

The main trader yelled out, "87!" He was frenetically writing down numbers on some papers, and the whole room—bankers and everybody—was yelling and screaming. The whole room was one giant "Waaaaa!" Everyone started howling; a few guys threw their phones down. All these heads popped up like prairie dogs; everyone was looking. It's total primal chaos.

They were all looking at me.

My first reaction was, "What the hell is 87?! Eighty-seven pesos?" Everyone laughed at me. They said, "No, 87 dollars."

Then five seconds later, someone screamed out, "$97!" Todd and I could only stare at each other, incredulously. The day before, we were at $9 and the deal was nearly dead. Now we're at $97. It took me a moment to realize we'd just become a $1 billion company.

Sweat was dripping off me, and my shirt was soaked. I could feel my body temperature soaring, the pressure building up to my head, and everyone was still yelling.

That was when the phones started ringing. A friend called to say, "*Ohmygod,* you guys are on CNN *right now.* Wait! You're on CNBC, too—it's breaking news." Everyone in the room was talking at once, and I heard myself getting hoarse. My throat was beginning to kill me.

The stock kept fluctuating. It flew between $97 and $60 within seconds. Boom, boom! Boom, boom! Up and down, 30 points up and down equaled a $300 million swing in market cap. It was just a wild fluctuation. All the institutions that had gone into the stock were dumping it like crazy. As soon as the stock would dip, somebody would buy in. To get a sense of how much action we generated, think about this: theglobe.com IPO was a 3-million-share deal. Sixteen million shares traded hands that day; everyone traded their shares at least five times over.

People we'd never met made millions because of us. Anyone who put a hundred grand down made $1 million. Even the traders at Bear Stearns were dumbfounded. We just set worldwide stock market history; no one had ever seen anything like this before. And we were 24 years old!

As we were heading over to the NASDAQ office for a press conference, an older trader, a gentleman in his nineties started tugging at my jacket. "Are you the guys who caused such a ruckus here today?" he asked. I nodded. "In my 40 years on Wall Street," he said, "I have never seen anything like this before."

Today, those words mean a lot to me.

Still, at the time I wasn't thinking about making history or that I was about to be running a billion-dollar company, but rather that I'd just extended our lease on life. Everything Todd and I had worked toward for four years wasn't exploding into a fiery ball. I didn't have to find a "normal" job.

I remember Michael turning to me and saying, "Well, enjoy it, boys. This is a really unsustainable number. It can't last."

Was *that* ever an understatement.

> > >

Whenever I meet people today, a lot of them say, "Hey, I know you. I saw you on CNN." Sometimes, they've seen me on MSNBC or CNBC or read about me in the *Wall Street Journal, Fortune,* or *Time.* It doesn't really matter, except that they always know who I am. "You're the kid who took that company public two years ago and set stock market history," they say. "You're the guy who was running a billion-dollar company at 24. You're the one who was worth $97 million dollars before your 25th birthday." Then they smile and say, "You're the guy who lost it all."

They're right, and this is my story.

> > >

My name is Stephan Paternot. Between 1994 and 2000, I was the cofounder and co-CEO of theglobe.com, an online community that I started with my former college buddy Todd Krizelman when we were both 20. On that fateful Friday the 13th in 1998, after four years of preparation—an adventure that began in the labs of Cornell University and culminated at the nexus of Wall Street and Silicon

Alley—theglobe.com went public up to $97 a share. I held a million shares. You do the math.

Fourteen months later, I watched in horror as the stock plummeted to $7, erasing my fortune almost as quickly as I'd managed to amass it. In August 2000, with the stock at $2, I formally stepped down as the chief executive of the company I founded.

I am proud to say that after seven years, theglobe.com is still in business at the writing of this book. But its rise and fall and the crazy era in American business history that theglobe.com ostensibly embodied has never been properly documented.

Until now.

Enjoy the ride.

PART 1

1

THE AMERICAN DREAM

I t all began with snails.

My first memory took place in our backyard in San Francisco where my mom would sprinkle snails on the hedges near the front lawn to churn the earth. Before I could even talk, I played in the mud with these slow-moving, slimy creatures. Playing with snails probably made me think I moved pretty fast.

I was born in San Francisco in 1974. Beyond the snails, I don't remember much more about the American phase of my childhood. There's a photo of me on the beach from that time, and I'm the little kid with a head three times too big for his body. And I'm completely blonde. The little kid in that picture seems like an imposter since my hair went to a very dark brown as I grew up.

After San Francisco, we moved to Switzerland, but getting there requires a brief detour. My dad is Yves Paternot, a Frenchman who graduated from Harvard Business School and cofounded Adia, which eventually became one of the largest temp companies in the world.

While he attended Harvard Business School, my mom—Mia Heineman—was at Boston University. After they met and fell in love, my mom dropped out; she never formally finished her degree. Once married, they moved to California so dad could start a U.S. branch of Adia, and shortly thereafter, Maddy, my sister, was born. Two years later, in 1974, I came along.

When I was four, my dad was transferred to Switzerland to set up the Swiss branch of Adia, and so we moved to Lausanne. This wasn't such a bad move for my dad since he'd be closer to his parents, who lived in Europe, but my whole American background was essentially erased overnight.

I was enrolled in Mont Olivet, a Catholic school in Lausanne. My teachers were nuns—and with nuns came rules. We had to follow the rules, like studying catechism every day, or else.

Lausanne is in the French-speaking region of Switzerland. Since I was only four (I'd stay until I was age nine), I essentially forgot whatever English I'd learned and French quickly became my preferred means of communication.

The entire Swiss population is less than 6 million people, and Lausanne is a tiny town near a large lake surrounded by the Alps. Approximately 250,000 people live there; everything is classic village life. Don't get me wrong. People love to vacation there. It's a beautiful little country. But the key word is *little.*

My problem with small-town life is the small-town mentality that comes with it. I'm sure that some Swiss people will be pissed at me when they read this, but here's the bottom line: It's a great place to retire (think Florida with mountains), but it's strange to grow up there. Even the presidential system is bizarre. One of the first things I realized about the society I grew up in was that they have six presidents who rotate into office every two years. So, if you ask Swiss citizens, especially young ones, who their president is, they rarely know. They actually don't know who their president is. I find this especially ironic since Europeans have such a good time making fun of Americans.

When I was eight years old, my mom and dad divorced after 11 years of marriage. This was during my fourth year in Switzerland, and at the risk of overstating the obvious, I'll say it was a tremendous event in my life. I remember crying, but for some reason thinking they weren't actual tears. I went through the motions of grief because that's what I thought I was supposed to do. But I actually felt happy about the fact that I was going to live with mom. I would be the man now.

My mom is a very liberated American woman. My dad is, you know, *French*. I think my mom went into the relationship loving my father, but hoping to turn him into the man she always wanted him to be. Of course, my dad entered the relationship never wanting to change anything.

> > >

After my parents split up, my mom, Maddy, and I moved to a small apartment. We'd been living in Lausanne in a nice house with a garage and a large garden. Thinking about it now, I don't think my mom had much money. She was supporting us with whatever money she'd inherited from her parents. We may not have had much money, but I enjoyed plenty of entertainment. I remember watching movies like *Condor Man* and *Raiders of the Lost Ark* in the local little Swiss theater. Even at this early age, I was open to creative influences, and what seemed like basic images to others were powerful visions to me. Meanwhile, my dad would visit as much as he could, bringing us gifts, new Walkmans, and other electronics that he picked up on business trips to Japan.

After living in Switzerland for five years, just as I was fully adjusting to speaking French, my mom told us we were moving back to the States. My dad, however, stayed in Switzerland and married my stepmother Monica; shortly thereafter, Eric and Sophie, my half-brother and half-sister, were born.

> > >

We moved to Greenwich, Connecticut, to a place called Lyon Farm, near where my mother grew up. In Switzerland, we'd been speaking franglais, a kind of pidgin French and English. In Connecticut, I had to start all over and learn English.

At this time my mom started dating. She briefly dated two chumps, and then she met Anders Bergendahl, a London-based Merrill Lynch banker who she's been married to for nearly 20 years now. Of course, I had no idea at the time they'd end up together for so long. All I knew was that this guy lived in London, and that was a long ways away. Mostly, I was pleased that she'd finally met a man she could love. But I was a lot less pleased that we were moving (again) to London.

And so, a year and a half after arriving in Connecticut from Switzerland from San Francisco, we picked up and moved to England. Of course, by this time, my English was a half-French, half-American hybrid-cum-disaster.

> > >

We lived in a narrow, dimly lit house in Kensington, right off Victoria Road. It was a cool house that looked like a run-down East Village walk-up in New York City, with a tiny garden. Not long after settling in, it was my mom and Anders's turn—soon David and Alexander, my next two half-brothers, were born.

My first few months in London were so scary. I went to a school called Hill House, which is an international school with a distinctly British flavor. The guy who ran it was an old British colonel. Everything was "Discipline! Righto, everyone!" I received cadet training with actual rifles. My fellow students had a lot of fun mimicking my

American-French accent. (When people are making fun of you, you prefer that they not be armed!)

I quickly noticed the major distinction between the American and the European school systems. In England, everything is handed to you on a platter but then force-fed down your throat. It's easy, since you don't have to make any decisions. But the reality is you don't have any choices.

Hill House was famous for making kids wear knickerbockers—little, red, puffy pants. You're just asking to be beaten up in the street. Then they add in a bright rust-orange sweater. We looked like we'd been rudely yanked from the pages of a Dickens novel. Every day we'd walk from the school, which is in Knightsbridge, up to Kensington Gardens in the most spastic uniforms ever seen. There we'd play soccer and rugby until our knees and feet were lacquered in mud—there were no gym outfits—and then come back to class all dirty and sweaty for the rest of the day.

The food was standard British crap. After a while, I began to get over the culture shock and started excelling at math. I was still very poor at writing, however. I'd never read the books like *Catcher in the Rye, Animal Farm,* and all the classics that are standard school reading. So I had never developed any idiomatic ease or analytical skills in English, and now they wanted me to read Shakespeare.

At 13, I was admitted to the City of London School, an all-boys British school where I'd stay till 16. My tenure at CLS wasn't helped by my unfortunate foot problem: flat feet. I had an operation to fix my right foot, and because of my bad feet, I couldn't wear regular shoes. I always had to wear sneakers. So I'm in this British school where everyone's in dark uniforms, and God, did I stand out in the crowd! I became known as the "kid with the white sneakers." Half the kids hated me because I had them, and the other half thought I was cool—the only kid who'd managed to break the rules.

At CLS, we had a choice of community service or combined cadet force. I opted for combined cadet force. What a moron! For two years, I did full military training. Not only did we practice during the week, but there were sessions during the year when we'd head to the countryside and suffer the indignity of nocturnal, self-reliance military training.

They used to drop us off 20 miles from our tents. We'd have 24 hours to get back to base camp. We had to carry 50-pound packs while wearing full military gear. Since I had to wear rigid military boots, my feet were bloody stumps.

> > >

In the sense that a British school is all about education at the expense of socialization, the City of London School was the worst of the worst. They forgot that we need to mature as human beings, too. Maybe these particular boys were so cruel and socially inept because they had no training in how to interact with females. We were 16 and completely clueless! I had to adapt—and fast.

It so happened that my sister was going to the American School in London, which sounded like a dream. First of all, it was co-ed. Plus, it was international, there were no uniforms, and you picked the classes that interested you. What a concept!

So at 16, I tested into the American School. It was 1990. Since my sister is a year and a half older than me, we were at that stage when brothers and sisters don't get along all that well. She and her friends were into older men, and I was the drooling younger brother. Inevitably, that awkward period began to close.

Meanwhile, in school I discovered computer science. Programming was particularly interesting to me. Until then, the only computer I ever had was a Commodore 64 with 64K RAM, and I used it to play some primitive cassette games. (There was one called "Chopper Command" I was very fond of.)

Now, all of a sudden, I'm sitting in front of these computers called Apples and I'm thinking, *What the hell are these?* At City of London School, I'd used these Brit computers like Acorn and Spectrum, but they were just pathetic pieces of equipment.

In the American School, I discovered the Macintosh and what a hard drive was. Then they started showing us these things called BBSs (Electronic Bulletin Boards) in the States, where you could call up America and "download" things. I got my first 300 baud modem; one night, I hooked up to the phone line for eight hours straight on a long-distance call to download a half-meg game. The phone bill was astronomical. My parents were not pleased.

I was fascinated by the whole concept of these BBSs. Back then, half the fun was trying to find the phone numbers to these exclusive clubs. There were ultra-elite BBSs, and you had to know someone who could get you in. And, of course, you couldn't download something unless you uploaded something. You had to earn credits so you could download. As I slowly turned into a geek, I started spending an alarming amount of time playing computer games.

During my first semester, I took Intro to Computer Science with Professor John Servente. This guy was incredibly quirky; you either loved him or you hated him. And if you loved computers, he loved you. Remember, we had just come out of the late 1980s when people were still asking, "Why the hell should I have to take a computer science class? I'm never going to use a computer."

While I was discovering Apples, I'd also discovered girls. Even better, I'd been told that a girl or two in school were actually convinced I was cute. As it happened, I ended up dating a very hot, very popular girl—Elayna. (Even her name was sexy.) We wound up going out for the following two and a half years, two of which would be a long-distance relationship.

How bizarre it was that I, Stephan Paternot, a computer geek who'd never known how to speak to a girl, became the envy of most of my male classmates. When I look back on the pride I had then, walking around with Elayna on my arm, I think, *How pathetic.* But back then, it made a significant difference to my whole perspective on life: It was the first sign that one could transcend the barriers of what one wanted to pursue, yet not be locked in as a one-track geeky engineer.

Anyway, as my computer science education evolved, I decided to push things further and take a programming class. From there, I moved into advanced programming—almost all in Pascal. The more I took, the more I got into it.

Back then, the visual manifestation of what I was doing was mainly a black screen with text scrolling up and down. I mean it was exactly like DOS. This was long before pointing and clicking.

Programming for me quickly became all about identifying a problem and deciding what to do about it. What did I want the machine to do? Then I'd backtrack my way from there. I sometimes worked on accounting systems; other times it was drawing. Sometimes it was just mathematical problems—extremely complex mathematical problems that required a computer to execute.

Programming for me just felt *good.* I liked being up at 4:00 in the morning, in my own little world where there were no limits to what I could do. I could make the machine change what it could do, do it faster, more efficiently, figure out these problems . . . problem *solving.* With physics, something I'd briefly considered, I could figure stuff out on paper, but there was nothing especially tangible to make. With a computer, I could get a glimpse of the future. In retrospect, I realize we were just coming out of the Dark Ages and I was watching it unfurl.

Aside from computer science, my only other interest, or skill I should say, was born out of my history and psychology classes. Unbeknownst to me, my teachers thought that my communication skills were good. I discovered this one day when my history teacher asked if I'd like to join the debate team. I was naturally surprised, considering I had changed languages and cultures so many times. I had become accustomed to living a somewhat shy and introverted life, and communicating or debating was the last thing I was interested in. Although I didn't join the debate team, I did elect to join the Model United Nations program in which students from all over the world fly to The Hague in Holland to represent countries in mock debates. On my first occasion, I represented Russia and amazingly passed my resolution for nonproliferation of nuclear weapons around the world. Presenting in front of 3,000 students was no piece of cake, but it was the first sign that I could speak well in public, and I loved it. This was the first inkling that there might be more to my life than just programming.

> > >

As I approached the end of high school, my next move—college—became a huge issue. I'd taken the SAT and scored a 720 in math and a 540 in verbal. Clearly, my math was stronger. My dad had always wanted me to study in Switzerland to be near him. He wanted me to go to The Polytechnic Federal School of Lausanne, a pure engineering program in a small town. I was opposed to this idea, but dad was adamant. He said, "Steph, I pay my taxes, which automatically gets you free university in Switzerland." For him, it was an opportunity to save a large amount of money. It was a good engineering school that was prepaid, and he definitely thought engineering was my thing. But I wasn't convinced. For the first time, I was discovering new horizons. I'd seen *Animal House* and all those other crazy stories about college life in America, and I wanted to have that experience. I wanted to be 10,000 miles away from the family, be alone to discover and experience life in an entirely different world (of course, you never realize the downsides—20/20 hindsight and all).

I was always reluctant to confront my dad. (I would oppose my mom, but not my father.) When and if I had to challenge him, my hands would be shaking with fear at the prospect. When he came to visit in London my final year in high school, we had another debate about my future, and I burst into tears, hating him for making it so difficult to tell him what I really wanted. I recall being in a restaurant with my dad and my stepmother Monica, and her saying, "Yves, let the kid speak." She understood that it's not always about winning. It's about . . . do you want to be loved for the rest of your life? Do you want your kids to look up to you for the rest of your life, or do you want them to hate you? I was in tears from frustration and nerves, and I felt betrayed in not being able to express myself openly.

I wanted to curse at him so badly. Do something that would insult him. But the last time I had done so resulted in a terrible scene for the both of us. I was much younger that time and had let a curse slip in the course of a conversation I was having with my dad. Out of reflex, he slapped me in the mouth, sufficiently hard enough that my lip split. I started bleeding all over myself. I started crying, feeling humiliated from being slapped, and my father was embarrassed by what he'd done. Of course, my father is not a bad man who liked to beat me. But a thing like that has a fundamental impact on you, especially when you're young. After that, I was never really very comfortable speaking my mind around him.

So the argument about college continued; I wanted to go to the States and my mom supported my decision to leave. I'd applied to Penn, Cornell, Tufts, and a few backup schools, and was admitted to most of them. I didn't get into Brown, which would have been my original choice. And so it came down to Penn and Cornell. I decided to attend Cornell because it was the better school for what I wanted to pursue.

My dad remained steadfast, "You're going to Switzerland."

I said, "No. This time I'm doing what I want."

I was on my way to Ithaca.

2

THE WORLD WIDE WHAT?

the origin of the internet and how two cornell
freshmen glimpsed the future

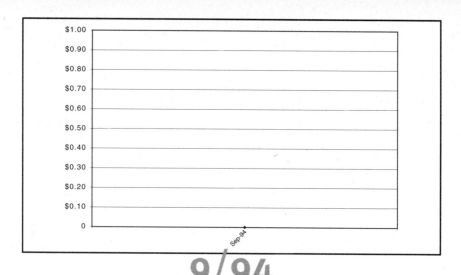

STOCK PRICE
(private company)

I arrived at Cornell in the fall of 1992. I was 18, fresh back from a one-month internship at the International Olympic Committee in Switzerland.

I remember wearing my standard British garb—a long leather jacket, a beanie (the hat, not the furry toy) that my sister gave me from a trip she'd taken to Morocco, and dark leather shoes with funky buckles. Everything about me sort of reeked London, to the point where people asked if I was "the guy from the U.K."

This was right when the United States was embracing grunge, and everyone seemed to be swathed in flannel. Coming from London, I had no idea what grunge was. To make matters worse, I'd begun growing my hair long. By the time I hit Ithaca, it was like some crazy weed that I arranged in a topknot with a rubber band.

Ithaca has always been well known for its gray skies. Simply put, 11 months of the year, it's gray—if it doesn't happen to be blizzarding. I remember my first day: all these people running around in red Cornell T-shirts, orientation counselors, people to welcome you, greet you, help carry your luggage to your dorm room. I quickly learned there was a west campus and a north campus. West was considered the cooler area; north campus was more geeky. I opted for a single bedroom dorm in the west side, as opposed to sharing with a roommate, so that Elayna could visit me.

I found myself isolated in a dorm called McFadden, a sinister old stone building. To get to my room, you had to climb this dark stone staircase to the third floor. My place had ancient little windows. Even when they were shut, a draft came in from the outside so that it was always freezing. My windows overlooked the tennis courts. Someone was always playing tennis. All day and night, *dink, dink, dink.* My bed consisted of a mattress on the floor; there was one minuscule closet. (I was now experiencing the downside of American college life!)

This was back in the day when having your own computer was just starting to become standard procedure. This was something of a surprise for a kid from the technological backwaters of London. I felt left out and isolated.

So one of the first things I did was to hunt around for a computer; I remember searching everywhere for something that was functional yet economical. The coolest computer at the time was the Power-Book, so I ended up with a 20 MHz Powerbook 145. It was one of those old rinky-dink Apple jobs, and I shelled out the extra cash so I could have a 40 meg hard drive—40 megs, not gig. Even then, memory was everything. But when you look back now, four megs of RAM and a 40 meg hard drive is just a joke. But it did have a cute little black-and-white screen.

I didn't know about Moore's Law at the time, but I quickly saw it happening when only six months later my fellow students had newer and more superior computers. To keep up, I convinced my dad to shell out $1,000 so I could buy myself a Centris 610, which had a 25 MHz chip. This was just infinitely superior and came with 16 megs of RAM. It was a speed demon, and I became the envy of a couple of new friends who'd bought their computers just before me.

The good computer helped me feel better adjusted, but those first few weeks were still unnerving. Then there was the nagging question of what I should actually be taking. For my first semester, I planned to major in environmental engineering. I'd seen a lot of programs about it, about the environment going to hell. I felt a minor calling, or at least I thought I did.

In my first environmental engineering class, we had to set up computerized flowcharts. We had to figure out, depending on the rate of river runoff and pollutants going in, how fast we could get rid of the pollution. Interesting in theory, but not for me.

It took just one semester for me to realize that I didn't want to pursue environmental engineering. Meanwhile, I was required to take freshman English, which meant Shakespeare. At this point, as I still wrote much better in French, I did terribly.

> > >

Slowly but surely, I made a few friends. Whilst I was sitting in my friend's dorm room one day, in walks this little guy who looked like he couldn't have been older than 14 or 15. I didn't know who he was, but he was certainly interesting looking: about 5′4″, short curly brown hair, brown eyes, and arms and legs hairy enough to match Robin Williams. I shook hands with the guy, and he introduced himself as Todd Krizelman. Then he let out this killer smile, a sort of Jack Nicholson as the Joker, grinning from ear to ear. It was a funny visage to my cartoonish brain, but you could tell this guy had real warmth of character, even a sort of perpetual happiness about him. But although I knew he was a college student and therefore must have been about 18 or 19, I still couldn't get over how young he looked. At the time that I met Todd, I was sitting on the lower tier of my friend's bunk beds. As it turned out, the bunk where I was sitting belonged to Todd, because he was the shorter guy.

Todd let me remain on his bed and went over to his desk, where he switched on his computer. My jaw dropped. Todd was probably the first guy in Cornell's history to own a PowerBook 180. I mean, this piece of gear was an order of magnitude superior to what I had. (And this wasn't even the only screen he had. He'd already hooked his active matrix laptop with 16 shades of gray to an external color monitor.)

Right away I started asking Todd about his gear, but he was pretty tight-lipped. He granted me 20 minutes to play one of his games. He seemed very organized, and it was clear he didn't like people messing with his stuff. Todd had this amazing flight game, a really smooth World War II fighter pilot simulator. I rapidly became addicted.

> > >

One evening, I was sitting in Todd's dorm room, playing with the flight simulator on his computer, when I noticed him taking out a little pack from his desk drawer. This was nothing out of the ordinary, until he opened the pack and pulled out a syringe right in front of me.

Two seconds later, he jabbed the syringe into a small vile, drew out some liquid, and stabbed himself in the waist with the needle. Then he turned to me with the needle in the air and said, "Now it's your turn." You should have seen my face. Then he smiled and said, "Only kidding. I'm a diabetic. I do this every day."

Because I'd never known anyone with diabetes, I spent the next few hours receiving a detailed lesson on what the disease entailed. By this time, Todd was a biogenetics major; he lived to give long-winded presentations of this stuff. What I found most fascinating—aside from the fact that he had to inject insulin several times a day—was this: If he didn't inject regularly or maintain body sugar at just the right level, he could end up in a coma, or worse, die. Then there was the fact that Todd also enjoyed telling me how easily insulin could kill an innocent bystander—and that there'd be no trace of what caused his death (think *Reversal of Fortune* with Jeremy Irons). Todd loved running up to me with syringe in hand, pretending to stab me. I didn't find this as amusing as Todd did! Of course, diabetes is nothing to laugh at.

> > >

Back to college days, Todd had taken a few computer science classes but very quickly discovered that he hated it. He couldn't program to save his life. Meanwhile, programming came so naturally to me that I ended up trading tutoring for more game time. Todd had one Pascal assignment in which he had to create an on-screen menu of different shapes—triangle, a square, a star. Not only did he have to draw those elements, but he had to be able to point and click on the screen where he wanted it to draw the shapes. It seemed pretty basic to me; Todd made it through the class with a C+. So we cut a deal. I would come and play his games, then I'd help him with his programming.

By the end of our freshman year, Todd and I were working in his dorm room so much we might as well have been roommates. In time I'd learn that he'd come from California, near San Francisco. He'd practically grown up with the Mac (which might explain his difficulty with programming), and computers were in his blood. Even with his love for computers, Todd couldn't quite get the concept of industry out of his mind. He once had his own printing business as a teenager and had even run his own magic show. He understood money. He was very frugal and was already into investing. In fact, he'd made some good money with Microsoft. Todd understood the business of the computers; I understood programming. I saw the potential for synergy. "Wouldn't it be amazing if we started our own technology company?" We both sort of laughed at the suggestion and left it at that.

In 1993, the United States was just beginning to come out of a recession. Bush had lost; Clinton was taking over. Living abroad, I'd only cared about the United States in terms of its impact on international politics. A U.S. student now, I noticed that my colleagues were groaning about their work prospects after college. The talk was very dispirited: It wasn't about picking the one thing you wanted—it was about finding anything.

This had a major impact on me. I'd have to start thinking about a career. I thought the obvious answer was to enroll in business school. Then I recalled something my father had told me: You can always become a businessman. If you want to be a Harvard MBA, great, but most companies like guys who've done some real-world engineering before, guys who have actual experience.

With this in mind, I backed away from business school during my second semester and stayed in engineering. But now, I would focus on computer science engineering. I plunged in full force and signed up for every available class. Besides, I'd been inspired by Cornell's job bulletin boards. Goldman Sachs and Merrill Lynch were looking for people in their information systems departments, and you could earn $53,000 a year. I remember that when I saw this I yelled out, "$53,000? That's huge!"

In the summer of 1994, I moved into a dilapidated apartment on Catherine Street that had a massive ant infestation. In addition, the doors were lopsided and the stove was faulty—it exploded in my face one day when I was cooking. The apartment was a death trap.

Literally.

I began noticing I was always ill, and I couldn't figure out why. One day I came home and discovered the heating was busted. When the gas company inspected the ancient heating system, they found that it was spewing 10 times the lethal level of carbon monoxide. And this had been the case for six months!

> > >

Engineering at Cornell was a tough major. Engineering used to be a five-year program; now they packed it into four. It helped if you did extracurricular study. I ended up spending all four summers at Cornell, taking extra classes just to stay ahead.

To simultaneously gain some so-called real-world experience while in school, I looked for an internship. I considered a sock company in New York that needed a computer network setup. Then there was a videoconferencing company called Datapoint, based in San Antonio, Texas. Videoconferencing sounded better than socks, so I decided to go to Texas. Plus, it wasn't so cold there.

Talk about feeling out of place. Here I am in cowboy country, still in my British-style clunky clothing, long hair, with a shoulder-length ponytail. After six months of working on software, I realized how much I absolutely did not want to be an engineer. When you're an engineer, you're sure that management is stupid because you have all these brilliant ideas. (Of course, management isn't completely stupid; they only see the dollar signs in what the engineers tell them.) I simply didn't want to be obsessing over minutiae late at night in my tiny cubicle and missing the big picture. I wanted to be in technology. But I wanted a place where I could see it from 10,000 feet up—from a vantage point where I could look down and see how the big picture was really progressing.

So . . . adios, Texas.

I bought a beat-up Toyota Corolla (my mom lent me the money) and drove all the way from Texas at 112 miles an hour—the maximum the car could do—with a radar jammer I'd built myself. I hauled ass through Baton Rouge, New Orleans down to Miami then up the coast to the dreaded Ithaca and somehow never got a ticket.

By this time, Elayna and I had been going out for two and a half years; the whole time we'd sustained this crazy long-distance relationship. Originally, she'd enrolled at Smith College, a few hundred miles away. After eight months, I finally convinced her to transfer to Cornell for a semester.

And so at the beginning of my junior year, Elayna arrived in

Ithaca. But, after two and a half years living in separate worlds, we got together and things promptly started falling apart.

I was miserable. I couldn't pull myself together. Elayna was my first major love, and now she became my first major breakup. I needed to get my mind off her and focus my energies into something productive, something big.

At the time, my sister Maddy had just graduated from Vassar. I used to go down to her place and hang out (and try to meet her friends). Liz, one of Maddy's best friends in NYC, had just received her first *Vassar Quarterly*, the school's alumni magazine. One afternoon, when I was sprawled on her couch feeling sorry for myself, I picked up the *Quarterly* and started distractedly reading.

That's where I saw a tiny column about this guy. I can't even remember his name. Actually, it wasn't even a column. It was just a blurb about a former student, letting people know what he was up to. The guy was selling T-shirts for the Helsinki Winter Games, shirts that more or less said, "Break a leg, Nancy" and other vapid slogans. Apparently, the shirts had sold so well that he'd received a call from some other guy who ran a Web site called Cybersight. They were going to sell the shirts on the site.

Now, at the time, nobody knew what a Web site was. Cybersight was supposed to be some "online Internet community," but there was no explanation. All it said was that the shirt guy and Cybersight were working together.

Here's all I knew about the Internet in the fall of 1994: It was this cryptic geeky arena in which he who can type "reverse back slash, forward slash colon" rules the world. And he who doesn't understand Unix can forget it.

Let me explain what was going on in the online universe at this point. AOL, CompuServe, and Prodigy already existed. They were the three commercial electronic companies, but they weren't exactly burning up the marketplace. This was back when they all charged $4.95 an hour. AOL in particular was having massive troubles; their stock had plummeted. No one knew where it was all going. A few players were struggling to set up an electronic world, but no one was really buying it. The companies had maybe a few hundred thousand subscribers. In the grand scheme of things, no one thought it was viable.

I'd been reading about these companies and knew the huge battles they were having with hourly rates. I knew how Steve Case had been struggling to raise money for his baby, and the trouble he'd had doing it. As a Mac person, I also knew that Apple had decided they were going to jump into this online fracas with something called eWorld.

So I picked up the *Quarterly* and I read about this site and all of a sudden something clicked: This theoretical universe called the Internet—which is a completely separate universe from AOL at the time—is partnering with old-fashioned marketing. I thought to myself, *Wait a second*. Is the Internet suddenly a viable medium for marketing? What does that mean? Is it going to instantly become user-friendly? Next to the blurb, there was a photo of two guys standing together, and for the oddest reason, I thought of Todd. I suddenly got so incredibly excited. I hopped back into my car and hightailed it up to Cornell.

I found Todd, and we plunged right in. I knew he was the guy to start a business with. We'd joked once about doing something in technology. Now we were serious.

> > >

Todd likes to draw schematics. Even now, he'll walk up to a board with some markers when we discuss things. He started drawing templates right off to see what this thing would look like. Then we decided to download Mosaic. Mosaic was the first program to marshal actual Web graphics (the word *browser* wasn't being used yet). With Mosaic, we'd heard, there was no such thing as background graphics. You literally had a gray screen with text on it, on which you could stick a picture at the top of the screen, left justified (since you couldn't even center it). There was something called an image map, where you could make pictures clickable, and you could actually get an image to take you to another link.

But this was before all these terms existed. Nobody knew what a URL was. Nobody knew anything. We didn't even know how to type in an address. Finding an address, finding a site to go to—it was virtually impossible. There were no directories. We found this thing called Yahoo, a tiny directory at Stanford. When we found them, they were still at akebono.stanford.edu.

But it took so long. Downloading was an ordeal. We used my lame Zoom 14.4 modem, and Todd's 19.2 modem, which was the best that possibly existed at the time. We started exploring these FTP sites, like at UMich, where they had a massive site for Macintosh users. (We were Mac all the way; Windows was such a cryptic environment. We were always laughing at their little C:> and those crazy paths to link software.)

So we went to the UMich Macintosh site and downloaded Mosaic. It was an 0.8 beta version. We didn't know how to use it; we just started screwing around. Finally, after we got a tiny handle on things, we went to Cybersight.

We couldn't find the dumb T-shirts, but we stumbled upon one of the first experiences Todd and I had with something called a chat room. We went to this chat room, figured out how to use it, then Todd hooked up his portable computer. We both logged into the same chat room, sitting right next to each other, and "talked" with each other—and with the 30 other people in the room.

It was primitive stuff. Basically, you'd write a message and hit Post. To see the message posted, you'd have to refresh the screen, refresh the screen, refresh the screen. You'd see other posts scrolling down the screen. There wasn't much to look at. Just a blank screen with a line of text and then a space, a line of text and a space, a line of text, and so on. Each line was attached to somebody's name, or handle, or whatever that was called. That was it. Then it was post and reload, post and reload, post and reload.

Still, it was addictive. We were corresponding with all these strangers, random people from around the world pretending to be someone else. We must have spent four hours on our first session. The experience was so exhilarating. For an instant I could glimpse the world ahead, the future, everything. It freaked me out.

But before I could utter a word to describe what I thought, that inkling was gone—the sense was so fleeting. I'd seen it, and now it was gone . . . but I knew that something was there. Todd and I were just giddy. It was insane. We didn't know where this was going, but we knew with complete certainty that it was the absolute beginning. Seeing the effect it had on us, we knew that when the world discovered this, there would be mania, absolute mania.

As the initial excitement faded, Todd and I looked at each other and realized we had to scramble. People were going to find this stuff. This was going to take on a life of its own. If we were not in the game, we would be out of it. We realized that if we wanted to do something, it would have to be now.

From that day, we began working together nonstop.

First, we had to figure out what the Internet was, what its capabilities were, and what the hell HTML was.

Every college kid likes to think he knows more than his professors. In a weird way, we did. Or at least we soon would. As recently as 1994, Cornell, that bastion of Ivy League edification, offered no courses in HTML. It simply wasn't taught. No one studied Mosaic; you couldn't learn it in school (my adviser would later end up teaching HTML and Java based on what we'd built with our company). We had to hunt for online sites with HTML resources.

We downloaded all sorts of documents about HTML and how to use it. We quickly discovered that it was the language that Web pages are made of. We both started trying to work the problem so we could get a feel for its capabilities. We tried to design our own chat room and created a hack version. It was bad, but you could really see the makings of something commercial.

> > >

Ah, money. For the first time, we faced the prospect that we could actually make money from what we were designing. We didn't know in what shape or form profit would take place (there was no such thing as Web-based advertising or commerce), but we knew there would be money to be made eventually—if eWorld and AOL were able to charge access fees, we knew there'd be something. We just had to figure out what that something might be. The problem was there were no standards, no rules.

We found out about Hot Wired, Wired magazine's Web site, but that didn't seem relevant. It was literally just a magazine online; we didn't have a magazine, and we couldn't start publishing or creating content. We had to think of something else. Chat seemed to be the thing—or at least the starting point. The addiction with chat was awesome, and we were increasingly certain that we could pursue a business in that world through some new sort of community.

We didn't even have a name for the company yet. We decided to call it Global Solutions, which later evolved into WebGenesis. Over the next couple of years, we would eventually abandon that and turn it into theglobe.com.

It was just the two of us. We had to figure everything out. One of the first things we realized was that we'd need seed money, which meant we'd have to write a business plan. We had no experience writing a business plan. We had no experience with business classes. We knew nothing. Nothing. Don't forget: We were two 20-year-old guys.

Ironically, one of the first things we discovered almost sunk us. The owner of Cybersight had published a decree in which he wrote,

"The Internet? Come on! That's never going to be commercial—an online mall will *never* happen." But we didn't give up.

Since we had no one to ask for advice, we called some guy in Boston who'd been writing and selling software. We thought maybe we could get some info from him about software for the Internet. We must have sounded so amateurish; this guy must have thought, *Why on earth are these kids calling me?*

We didn't know how to speak like professionals. I mean, we sounded like two students trying to latch on to someone. People were probably just as wary of us as we were of them. We decided we'd just have to do this ourselves.

So we started working on a business plan. Like any good business, we needed a motto. During the summer, Todd had been interning at a biotech company whose motto was To Please and to Satisfy. So that became our motto, too. To Please and to Satisfy. It sounded brilliant, so we put it in our business plan. Why not, right?

We wrote a 14-page business plan, the most important part of which was the cream-colored paper with a nice font, a good cover, and a great binding. Todd and I were so proud of the way it looked (never mind the substance).

We had snapshots of what our site would look like. Since Todd and I were such Mac fans, we decided it would look like eWorld, Apple's pride and joy. We decided that you'd click on different areas and get little zoom diagrams. There'd be a newsstand where you could get news, and there'd be a little cafe.

That was the thing for us. If we created virtual cafes where people from around the world could get together, they could talk and have virtual coffee. So we described that, and that was the business model. We were so naive.

As we continued our work, Todd did the graphics, and I worried about programming and the technical aspects.

There was still no such thing as page impressions; the only term that had vaguely begun to exist was *bits*. "How many hits are you getting?" Slowly, we learned about the growing interest in advertising, so we added all sorts of research about ad rates based on how traditional media worked. That would be the way we'd make money.

Around this time, my dad happened to be coming to the States. When he arrived, I showed him our magnificent business plan. He opened it up, and the whole binding fell apart. It was pathetic. Not a great first impression. Then he read the motto, To Please and Satisfy.

"*Hmmm*. Did you come up with that, Steph?"

> > >

The good part was that he read it and was actually supportive. But he didn't seem overly excited. And who could blame him? He'd never heard of the Internet. There was no real business behind this business plan. He must have thought, *That's nice, Steph, but make sure you get your degree and don't lose focus on your studies.* As I mentioned, when I was growing up in Europe, I barely used a computer. My parents *never* used computers. They didn't even know where the on/off switch was, and there I was trying to talk to them about a virtual online community. It was total blind faith.

The proposition for theglobe.com, which Todd and I slowly got better at explaining, was the concept of community. It wasn't just a directory of sites, like Yahoo. We were all about being a destination site. That's the term we used. We wanted to be a destination. We'd be one of the places people would click to from a search engine to visit and stay and spend time there.

Our families would ask, "How do you get people to spend time?" We explained, "We'll have them read comics or download software and games. We'll have them hang out in the chat rooms. Most important, we're going to get people to meet other people. Because if they meet at our place, the common bond becomes each other.

Then we don't have to worry about spending tons of money to keep people interested with other bells and whistles."

They had no clue what we were talking about.

But they went with it. If anything, they must have thought it would make for an interesting experience. My mom, dad, and Anders each put in $500. My grandfather put in $500. Other people I talked to put in a little bit of money, and it added up to $7,500. Todd raised the same figure. We returned from Christmas vacation early and headed straight back to the dorm. Now we had $15,000, enough to get started.

In the beginning of 1995, we first heard that Jim Clark and Marc Andreesen had rechristened Mosaic Communications to Netscape Communications. From that day on, we felt the first sense of real heated pressure. This Web thing was starting to generate genuine companies. If there was one, there'd soon be a hundred.

The time came for us to come up with a budget. "Okay," we said, "we'll need a color scanner. We'll need another computer. We'll need all this gear." It looked like that $15,000 might not be enough.

Todd and I started looking at the backs of magazines for those tiny used-gear ads. We called everybody. We became master negotiators. "How much can we get for this eight meg SIMM of RAM? 150 bucks? How 'bout $145?"

Ultimately, we got the gear we needed to start our baby up.

Meanwhile, we were still taking classes. Every time we had a free second, we'd rush back to the dorm to meet up and talk. It was hard to excel as a student. Even when we were sitting in class, we weren't really paying attention. Our minds were flying with the possibilities.

My grades started suffering. I'd never been a really heavy study, but this was ridiculous. To get by, I started engaging in that all-too-common college habit, *um*, copying. Once, in Econ 101, a lecture hall class with 3,000 students, I walked over and took several assignments out of an in-box up front to "borrow." Even so, I ended up falling to a B average.

As I was skating by in my classes, I was building the tools for a barely born technology, making the stuff up as I went along. What I was doing seemed like a combination of computer science and electrical engineering. I was teaching myself about bandwidth, and bit rates, and all these other things that, until then, I would have never understood.

The time came for Todd and me to stop working out of a dorm room, but what were we going to do about the way we were desperately falling behind in our classes? What could we do? Then we had a brainstorm. And, like a god, one of my advisers accepted our idea.

We'd create an independent project—something that we could get actual credit for. All we had to do was come up with a thesis they would accept. Now, while we were secretly laying the groundwork for a new business, we'd also officially be studying the benchmarks of hard drive performance. In other words, we would test to see how hard you could push a computer before it exploded (which was kind of fun). And thus was born Independent Research CS490. Four credits per semester. Praise the Lord.

Now we were free to set up an on-campus office. We found this fourth-floor storage room, a cramped dust trap where the university stored all sorts of boxes and old stuff, and in March 1995, we convinced them to let us turn that into WebGenesis (the corporate name we still went by) World HQ.

The storage room was completely windowless. There would be days when we would go in there at 9:00 A.M. and leave at 3:00 A.M., and suddenly there'd be a foot of snow outside. To make the place more palatable, we moved the boxes aside, put up some filing cabinets, and divided the room in half. The place always smelled very . . . stale.

Maintaining secrecy was a major issue. We were risk averse to the point of paranoia. Even if the university didn't care what we were doing, Todd and I had heard stories about schools belatedly taking credit for intellectual property created on their turf. So we kept our mouths shut and continued faux testing those hard drives.

> > >

In January 1995, Todd and I had come to the conclusion that we could no longer build this company by ourselves. Shortly after we moved out of Todd's dorm room and into the windowless storage room, we decided to hire our first few employees. Of course, we didn't have a human resources (HR) department or a recruiting office, so we decided to do the most logical thing we could: place ads in the Cornell campus papers.

At the time, Todd and I were 20-year-old juniors. It seemed practical to hire people with experience. We put out several ads that read, "Looking for seasoned management, must be at least Junior or Senior."

Shortly after running the ads we received dozens and dozens of responses. There was just one problem—we didn't know where to interview these candidates. We didn't think it would make a good impression to bring prospective employees for a first meeting in a windowless closet, so we opted for the more elegant campus space called Willard Straight Hall. This Cornell landmark is an ornate hall with a 50-foot ceiling, beautiful stained-glass windows, plush red fabric, and a grand piano at the end of the hall.

Todd and I brought in three folding chairs and plopped them down in this great empty hall and called in our interviewees one at a time. Every 20 minutes, we'd call in the next person and go through a checklist: what year, what's your degree, do you use a computer, have you heard of the Web, what do you like to do on the Web, and so on. The best candidates were the ones who spoke about how they loved to go online and download stuff in their spare time, people who did this stuff for fun and liked the idea of getting paid to do it. The last thing we cared about was good grades. At this stage of the game, it was less about IQ and more about EQ, emotional quotient. We wanted people with character, people who were motivated, people who would want to work lots of late nights for nothing more than minimum wage because they enjoyed what we were doing.

Looking back now, given the HR department we set up over the ensuing years, these first interviews seem like a joke. But at the time, Todd and I took them very seriously. Most of our questions could probably barely be heard above the clamor of whoever was clanging away on the piano. Still, we managed to hire our first half-dozen employees this way, even if they became deaf in the process.

Our first employee was Philip Karlson, one of my computer science buddies. Philip had long, long blonde hair down to his butt; he had a Thor's hammer as a necklace; he made funny goat noises and drank massive pitchers of beer. He was also a great programmer.

Philip began setting up the servers, programming in AppleScript and C++. He was the guy who really programmed our first chat room and (almost) got it working. Since we spent most of our 15 grand on gear, we could only pay Philip $4 an hour, plus lots of pizza and beer.

When we first started setting things up, we used to work so long and hard that we'd occasionally reward ourselves by taking the servers down and dig into long sessions of "Marathon" (the Mac equivalent of "Doom"). There'd be lots of yelling and screaming. Eventually, we'd hear a knock on the door and there'd be some poor professor telling us to be quiet or we'd be kicked out. We'd say, "Oops, sorry," then put the servers back up.

That spring we were almost ready to go. We got the site up and running but hadn't publicized anything so there was no traffic. We had our home page. Then we also decided to be a mirror for software. So we copied over all the software from UMich onto our servers, making our site an eclectic mix of chat room and downloadable software. That was the best we could do. We had no idea what people would like—not a clue. But we pressed on.

Our second employee was Vance Huntley, who became our top programmer. Vance's previous experience was as a falafel cook at Aladdin's, a local health-food joint. He'd sort of dropped out of school for the moment. He'd been studying to be a high-energy particle simulation physicist. I mean, we're talking advanced theoretical computational calculation stuff.

Vance came on board. Between us and falafels, he was working 90-hour weeks. The guy was just deathly pale. Every day we thought he was going to walk in and collapse. Which is exactly what he eventually did. I remember he started bleeding from his nose at one point. "Oh, my God, Vance!" we said as he stumbled out the door, "You've got to recuperate."

Then we found Garth. He was a big oafish, hippie type who drew comics. We wanted a strip because it seemed like a good way to develop a following. After all, Netscape had this character called Mozilla, a little green lizard, on its home page. Wherever you went, there was this little character, and since you were always getting lost in the early days of the Web, it was a great way to identify what site you were looking at—a branding tool.

So Garth developed a comic strip for our site called "The Adventures of Net Surfer and Glitch." Net Surfer was a cool, blonde dude on a surfboard, and Glitch was a purple gnome with little antennae and a big nose. Then there was the evil Megabyte and a goofy character named Main Frame. These guys temporarily helped define what would soon become theglobe.com.

> > >

We launched the site on April 1, 1995—April Fools' Day. Probably not the best timing given that a lot of people thought it was a joke. Nevertheless, somehow people started coming. Right away, the chat room was the main attraction. People just started flocking into it. We'd made it extra cool by using those support icons, which was our big breakthrough; instead of just having a string of text, you could pick an icon to represent you. The icons, of course, were the characters from our comic strip. You could be Net Surfer, or you could be Glitch. Believe it or not, this was innovative at the time. Our chat really took off. You could literally watch the surfers as the traffic soared. It would climb and climb and climb, and we'd all hold hands and shout, "Yes!"

In the first month, we got 3,000 users. In the second month, it went up to 15,000 users. And the third month, it was 30,000. Then it got up to 45,000. Month after month, it was just climbing all by itself. We weren't advertising at all. This was strictly word-of-mouth.

Now we could demonstrate that our traffic over the first four months had ballooned. The usage time had gone way up. Our chat rooms were constantly filled. There were almost no other chat rooms on the Internet you could find that were always filled, but ours would have 30 people in a room chatting away at 4:00 in the morning. At prime time, there would be 200 people simultaneously chatting. We had continuous chatter.

Obviously, we could see the commercial potential. The time had come to bring in advertisers. But how? Then there was the issue of bringing in new investors—we were running low on funds again. That's where we found ourselves as we approached the summer of 1995.

That May in 1995, we officially named the site theglobe.com and incorporated the company as WebGenesis. Working with our parents and a team of lawyers they helped set us up with, we addressed the question of valuation. One lawyer said, "You could argue that this thing is worth a quarter of a million." Todd and I were like, "What? Our project worth a quarter of a million? Holy Moley!"

Of course this was a completely arbitrary enterprise value. But at this point, to get anyone beyond family to put money in, we had to have a real value so that people knew they were getting into something official. And we really needed money. We'd been hearing about other companies, like Lycos, that were aggressively raising capital. We could no longer think of ourselves as a little project.

We set up a Subchapter C corporation, incorporated in Delaware, and went with the value of about a quarter of a million dollars. What we didn't know was that in California, where baby Web companies were opening left and right, they were going with values of at least $1 to $10 million.

This was also around the time when we first heard whispers that Netscape was going to file to go public and that they were going to be valued in the hundreds of millions. The numbers were astral. Todd and I knew that we were onto something big and we'd now be compelled to raise a lot more money if we intended to play in the big leagues. Yahoo had already secured about $750,000 in financing from Sequoia (a venture capital outfit), even though they were still a project at Stanford. After that, they'd decided to move off campus. Jerry Yang and David Filo were dropping out of their Ph.D. programs, which they were about to complete. (When we first launched theglobe.com, we'd e-mailed Jerry and David to put us in their search engine. They replied, "Sure, no problem.")

Todd and I started debating. "Should we blow off Cornell? Do we drop out?" Our parents said, "Hold on a second." We were torn. Maybe we should hold on. Ultimately, we decided to try and graduate—even if it killed us. We might finish late, but we were going to continue taking our classes. My junior year was just a horrendous workload. This is where you face the real meat of computer science, and I was just miserable; I was taking five classes, all high-level computer science, but I stuck with it.

At this point, we'd barely managed to secure another $30,000— again, mainly from friends and family. It wasn't anywhere near enough money, but it was just enough for us to move off campus and look for real office space in Ithaca. Altogether, with temps, we had about 10 people working for us now, and we were seeing more than 50,000 users a month. Working with other people's money created a sense of responsibility and reality. In a few months, we'd morphed from an experimental dream into the real thing.

We were 21 years old.

We had no idea what lay ahead.

3
THE EARLY DAYS

paying in pizza and minimum wage
and the hunt for vc dollars:
ten meetings, ten rejections

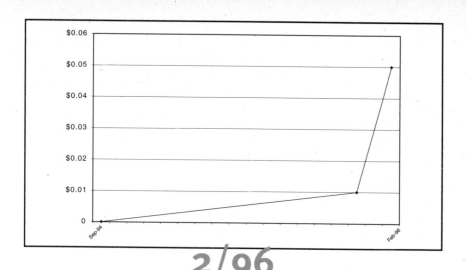

2/96

STOCK PRICE
(private company)

I n the summer of 1995, we moved off campus to College Town, into our crappy little corporate office in the Student Agencies building on College Avenue. We wanted it to be perfect, meticulous, beautiful. So we lined up the computers in a straight line. It was a start.

In order to make the rent and cover the employees we hoped to hire, the first thing Todd and I had to do was raise more money.

This was a process we'd soon become experts in.

We started in the early summer, putting informal financials together and talking to my dad. The idea was that with another $30,000 we'd be "there."

Then my dad said, "Well, Steph, why don't you work out what you really need for a longer period of time rather than just the minimum?"

For Todd and me, this was the first time we'd ever heard about raising more money than the minimum we actually needed to get by. *Hmmm,* interesting concept.

So, we started beefing up the financial plan—maybe we should go for $50,000? $60,000? Maybe we won't even cap it. Maybe we'll just keep increasing the amount of money we're trying to raise until such a time as we've gotten enough.

That summer, Todd and I started traveling back and forth to the West Coast, a frequent journey that would continue into the fall and well beyond. When I look back at the time between 1995 and 1997, it seems like most of it was spent raising money.

You have to remember that this was not an easy time to raise money. No one really understood what the Internet was. Every time we met a potential backer, we had to backtrack through the whole "Let's talk about the Internet and what it is" spiel and explain why this was indeed a viable medium.

We made our initial moves out of Todd's house in Atherton, California, which is just south of Palo Alto. But we really did most of our setup work in Kinko's, printing up business plans, making corrections; then we'd set up meetings. Todd's dad happened to know a few venture capitalists on the West Coast. We cold-called all the other investors. We went to Sudder Hill Ventures. We went to Kleiner Perkins Caufield & Byers (KPCB), Greylock, Crosspoint Ventures, and many, many more. We had no idea what we were doing.

Todd and I had never pitched before. The whole process was a complete trial by fire—how to pitch and modify your business plan as you go along. From an original 14 pages, we were revising the plan every two months, bulking it up with more industry background, competitive analysis, detailed financials, management bios, traffic statistics . . . all the new essentials, whilst also describing all the software tools we'd developed and hyping theglobe.com.

Mainly, we got blank faces. Internet mania still hadn't hit. A few people knew that Netscape had raised $5 million after a 30-minute meeting with Kleiner Perkins. But most people were still on the periphery. This was back in the day when VCs only knew technology companies. Everything was about software and hardware. Venture capitalists weren't into investing in games or entertainment. They'd classically always stayed away from the entertainment sector such as film, media, and the things you can't think about in terms of product upgrades, new versions, and distribution channels. When we arrived out there, the only real response we got, if any, was, "Okay, talk to us about these tools you guys are developing."

>   >   >

By late summer, we were leaning toward describing theglobe.com as a community and we were thinking about this as a media play. That would be the bigger potential. We had these chat rooms, which had taken off. We had this massive activity and addiction. On the other side of business were these tools, which we were only interested in selling as a way to make quick cash up front—we really didn't think it would be a great business to be in.

Still, for the VCs, tools were the only things they seemed able to latch onto. People would say things like, "This chat room you've developed . . . You guys ever thought about doing it in Java and then licensing that out?" or "What about your registration software? Your survey tools?"

We took hundreds of these meetings. They're not exactly a barrel of laughs. You sit there; you have an hour. They *look* interested. Todd and I would look at each other, wink-wink, nudge-nudge. We'd think things were going pretty well. Then the meeting would end, and we'd get the ol', "We'll get back to you . . . this is all *very* interesting."

Then we'd never hear back from them. A big problem was our ages. If Todd and I had been two gray-haired geeks with thick-rimmed spectacles fresh out of Microsoft, it would have been a done deal. But who could blame them? Would you do business with two baby-faced 21-year-olds?

And we could barely pass for 21. I looked maybe 20, and Todd looked even younger. When we walked into meetings, the VCs always had this expression like, *Oh, my God. Can we possibly even consider this?* VCs like to invest, at minimum, in quarter-million to half-million increments, but they prefer $5 million lumps. They would look at us as if thinking, *These kids can't even handle a quarter-million-dollar investment.* At first, they were probably right.

Our other problem back then was that the VCs were extremely geographically focused. They would only invest in companies that were in San Francisco, particularly in the Bay Area, so that they could be within an hour from their money.

Then here we come—not just from the other coast, but from Ithaca, New York. Upstate, the boonies. This was simply a no-go. Meanwhile, we couldn't find any VCs in New York City. At the time, 99 percent of the industry was based in San Francisco. Not to mention the difference in mentalities: East Coast investors were much more involved in high finance and banking; West Coast VC was about constantly digging for nifty new technologies.

And the guys who followed those companies were just starting to see the potential of a pure, highly efficient electronic world where everything moved at the speed of light. That season, you could feel the global aspects coming into play—hemisphere versus hemisphere. Still, the Internet was tiny at the time. When we went online, there were somewhere between 5 to 10 million users worldwide. But it was doubling month to month. It was growing exponentially, and we were right there from the beginning to watch it.

So we stayed with the left coast, where the minds were a bit more open, and things finally happened.

By mid-1996, Yahoo, Excite, and Lycos had gone public. Each had raised $30 to $35 million at $150 to $200 million valuations. They'd all gone public at anywhere between $15 to $20 a share; within six months they were trading at $2 to $7 a share. Internet mania didn't exist yet. It would be a full year to a year and a half before their stocks all started taking off like speed-fueled bulls. Only then did people really start saying, "Oh, maybe I should get some Internet stock. Maybe this Net thing is really something."

One day we found ourselves through a series of lucky breaks in a meeting with Bob Halperin, the former CEO of Raychem, the multi-billion-dollar material sciences company. Bob, a guy who you might—mistakenly—call an old paradigm, seemed to instantly take us under his wing. He was recruited in World War II as one of the five greatest brains working for the Pentagon as a strategist. In other words, a brilliant guy. Todd and I sat down and pitched him. We'd get so excited that we'd finish each other's sentences. Bob asked, "You boys always interrupt each other like this?" He's got this warm, gravelly voice that's very contagious. "I love the energy you have," he'd tell us. "You gotta clean it up a bit, but it's fantastic. It feels like you guys are real believers."

Bob looked at our numbers and showed us how we could ramp things up to a million in revenue the next year, and then to $2 and then $3 million the following year. Bob said, "Boys, to really interest venture capitalists, you need to show 5 to 10 times the revenue growth you do." Todd and I realized it was time for a quick modification of the plan. Bob invested $100,000 and became our first board member.

Now the plan was to do $1 million. Then we would do $10 million. Then $30 million. We just instantly curved it up. What else could we do? With those numbers down on paper, he was willing to personally make us a few introductions.

One guy Bob set us up with was Vinod Khosla of Kleiner Perkins, a quintessential entrepreneur well known on the West Coast. Now, VCs like to outdo each other in the way they manifest their power—it's a White House thing. They want you to feel that you're on this hallowed ground, that you're entering the domain of the mighty. When we walked into the KPCB offices on Sand Hill Road, we passed through this massive doorway with huge wooden beams.

Inside, there's a cavernous room with an enormous glass wall. We were impressed. The day we walked in, there were other investor meetings under way, and we just knew that those heavies behind glass could raise a half billion in one shot.

KPCB is considered the Ivy League of venture capitalists. Everyone knew that they were the best. And that was certainly what they thought of themselves. Todd and I were in total awe.

Not that you could tell from how we dressed. We always wore casual clothing. Todd wore khakis and a button-down shirt. I wore jeans and a T-shirt. You have to remember that, despite the setting, we were still two college students with no money, living in an absolute dump. It's not that we chose to skip the suits—we just didn't have any.

I suppose we could have borrowed a suit. But just as KPCB was a well-known firm, it was quickly becoming equally well known that young kids were driving the new Net business. We wanted them to see that we were in touch. In fact, it was the guys in suits who generated more suspicion when they pitched Net business. The VCs were skeptical that anyone in a suit actually used the Net. In our case, there was no doubt we were plugged in.

Still, we were sweating bullets when we met Vinod. This guy was tough. He grilled us about our business. There was a board on his wall with charts and all these comparisons to other Net companies. "Do you boys have a chat?" he asked. "What can your chat do? Okay, it's Java. What features do you have? Is it 3-D? Do you have icons? Do you have this, that, and the other?" He'd start talking about all the other little start-ups he'd heard of on the West Coast. There was one 3-D chat set up with streaming audio that had just received a $23 million investment. These were just insane sums, and here was Vinod comparing us to them.

So, we'd proceed through endless meetings. They'd basically be two hours of nonstop pitching—our chance to raise the money that could make or break the whole company. The force of energy we put into it was mind-boggling. But to little avail. Vinod had a famous line he loved to trot out, "At Kleiner Perkins," he'd intone, "we don't just create companies, we create industries." But maybe we had the making of an industry. Even though we were a tiny player with 50,000 users compared to Excite's (one of Vinod's proudest investments) 3 million, we were indeed beginning to be known in the community sector.

Adding another wrinkle to our worries was the sudden arrival of genuine competition. Other companies that were barely out of the box were proclaiming themselves community, too. They were raising a ton of money and generating the hype and the buzz. Todd and I were really bitter about that. It pissed us off, but it also made us all the more excited. As a result, we'd put this massive pressure on ourselves to hurry up and get there. Still, every time we'd think we had Vinod's money, our meetings would end with him saying, "Thanks for the update, boys." *Arrgh!*

Ultimately, Vinod passed. But he liked us and wanted to see if he could set something else up. Vinod introduced us to the guys at Excite, which would have been a fantastic relationship. But very quickly, Excite began referring to us as "the boys from theglobe.com." They wouldn't take us seriously. Ironically, that's how most of our VC meetings went. All our discussions kept ending with, "Why don't you guys sell your chat? Why don't you sell your software?" It would always be the same song—and that wasn't going to cut it. We could have sold our software, but it wouldn't be valued much more than at $10,000 per system. We had a registration system. We had cool chat software. We had survey software. This could have brought in money. It could have been our bread and butter. But even then we knew the bread and butter would be tiny. And after a while, we'd grow malnourished on bread and butter.

Besides, if we went into the software business, we'd just be crushed by Microsoft whenever they decided to make our stuff a little bit better. Todd and I debated it for a while, and we decided once and for all that we'd place our bets on the site itself. It seemed so much more exciting. Let's call it a media play and just go for broke on that. Besides, Todd and I wouldn't even know how to manage a software licensing business.

Still, by the end of our first trip out west, we only managed to raise a paltry $100,000.

Then we met David Horowitz. David had been the founder and former CEO of MTV. He happened to sit on the board of daVinci Time & Space with Bob, which was developing next-generation CD-Roms (back when CD-Roms were all the craze). Besides his business experience, David had another great asset going for him: He was based on the East Coast. Todd and I knew this was a fantastic opportunity.

As soon as we got back to Ithaca, David called. "I've heard of some project you're working on," he said in this comically loud baritone. "How 'bout a meeting?" These guys always have booming voices. You sit there thinking about the powerful industries they've run, and you can feel the hairs tingling on the back of your neck with the prospect of getting together.

When David called, Todd and I were sitting in our tiny office. We could barely squeeze into our desks, which were two feet away from each other (a detail that actually ended up being a major problem).

After David made it clear that he really did want to meet with us, Todd and I got in my Corolla and drove to New York at 95 miles an hour. My Corolla was in bad shape. Every time it took a left turn, the freezer coolant in the air-conditioning would pour onto the passenger's leg. We had to take turns driving because it was complete agony.

David had an apartment on the Upper East Side in a doorman Park Avenue building. It was one of those apartments where you could tell the resident had achieved a lot in life. It felt *money*, baby—well furnished, nice art, etc. The elevator opened right onto his floor. We said "hi" to his wife and then went into this handsome office packed with books.

At this point, David was one of the few execs actually using the Net. He would log on and everything—it was quite amazing. He had a 28.8 modem, which was twice the speed of anything Todd and I had.

There was this amazing picture of him holding a statuette that said MTV and VH1, taken shortly after he'd started the whole thing up. It seemed like a perfect match. David was clearly someone who understood media. We could learn so much from this guy. David realized that theglobe.com's model was in many ways like MTV—they really didn't make any money from subscription fees. It was all advertising based.

After a sweaty and intense meeting in which we pitched like maniacs—we'd started to get pretty good at it—he said, "Guys, I'm in for $50,000." Between David, Bob, and a few other angel investors, we cumulatively raised about $600,000 and managed to close our second round of financing. Now we could say Bob and David were on our board. Back then, when nobody really understood anything, it was all about who invested, who sat on your board. Naturally, we were thrilled, especially since the checks we were writing to our employees were practically bouncing.

> > >

As a young businessman, there's a lot to learn on the fly. In the early days, when we were constantly battling for financing, we were extraparanoid about competition. We didn't know how to manage a business, so we operated like a little clandestine operation.

We never told our employees what our financial situation was. We thought that they'd be scared sh*tless if they knew we had almost no cash. We never even told them we were raising money. We'd only tell them once we had closed a round. "Hey, guys, we got some more money," and they'd say, "really, we were raising money?" In fact, during those first few years, our employees had no idea of the stress Todd and I were undergoing, most of which had to do with one simple fact—we were not making money.

Any profit Todd and I had made at this point was through the buying and selling of our software. In late 1995, we landed our first story in *MacWEEK*. *MacWEEK* was mainly writing about the Macintosh world; they were not yet addressing the Internet. Still, they wrote about our tools. When that happened, people started coming to the site and buying the software. So when we met with VCs, our financial model was based partly on what it would look like if we could sell advertising on the site and what it would look like if our software tools took off.

Very quickly, we started having formal board meetings and promoted this new strategy. Todd and I established a pattern: We'd haul ass from Ithaca to NYC in my car, meet for an hour, and go over the details of our business. Sometimes we were just feeding updates to David.

When Bob came to the meetings, he would fly in on the red-eye from San Francisco. He'd show up in a trench coat, wheeling around his two pieces of luggage, fresh off the subway. "Bob, you're a billionaire," I'd say. "What are you doing on the subway?"

Amazingly, neither of them ever condescended to us. I think they genuinely respected that we were on the cutting edge, at least in terms of understanding this emerging market. For them—and, to me, this is an amazing American concept—business is a culture bred on making your money and then reinvesting it into other people who have great ideas. You invest in older people, middle-aged people, and young people.

At our meetings, Todd and I would give all sorts of statistics on traffic; everything was growing fast. Of course, as I said, we weren't really making any money. I don't know how Todd and I got away with it, but for two years we managed to give Bob and David updates that never really showed revenue growth. They were growing, but in tiny increments. And not from software. In fact, by the end of 1995, Todd and I had entirely abandoned the software thing. As we went into 1996, it was a whole new ball game.

We had reached the critical mass of 100,000 users. This was a major watermark. Major. Once, we'd met with Apple Computers on the West Coast. Apple's abortive eWorld community was still up; they had about 75,000 subscribers. I remember them telling us, "You know, it's going to be tough for you guys to make money on this unless you get to the 50,000 user mark." (Later, we'd have more than a quarter million monthly users, whereas eWorld only got up to about 50,000 to 75,000 subscribers and then just gave up.) Now we had twice that, and we knew users were something we could profit from. Around this time, we met Kevin O'Connor, founder of Double-click—the first online advertising network.

Slowly but surely, the Web advertising craze started to happen as banner ads standardized and suddenly became the rage. Advertising, we decided, would be theglobe.com's business.

So we signed up with Doubleclick, and they put their banners on our site and distributed ads. All of a sudden, Todd and I were making $20,000 a month, $30,000 a month, $40,000 a month, $50,000 a month. In October 1996, we hit $85,000 a month in revenue, and our costs were only $50,000 a month. It was the most amazing feeling. We could actually go to the board and say, "Guys, we had a month of profitability." We could show real growing revenues. The board was superexcited. This was particularly amazing, since we only had about 12 to 15 employees—and we paid them nothing.

Still, Todd and I realized that we had to get bigger to survive. So, reluctantly, in late 1996, we went back once again on the financing circuit. Since we'd never really received any substantive VC money, the only alternative for us was to go after individuals and angel investors, but this time we weren't going to rest until we hit the millions.

It was a wild ride. At one point, there was interest from the owner of a winery in upstate New York. Todd and I got in my Corolla, drove an hour and a half up to a winery, and sat down to a wine-tasting with the owner, simultaneously pitching her and sniffing bouquets. The owner listened quietly and finally said, "Yes, I'd be interested in investing. I might be able to put in $25,000 to $50,000." Hallelujah!

A couple of weeks later, she wasn't interested. She didn't understand the Net.

Another time, we met with a private investor based in Florida (Todd and I were always skeptical about Florida). This guy ran all sorts of bizarre enterprises (he was heavily involved with a deep-sea, treasure-hunting operation). He started throwing around numbers. At one point, he said, "I'm prepared to invest $7 million in this puppy."

Joy.

There was just one problem: Every time we worked up a financing deal, we'd raise the future stock price (we were still a private company). Mr. Florida was willing to put in $7 million, but it would have to be at a massive stock discount. Todd and I hit the brakes. This guy would have eaten up 90 percent of our company—for $7 million.

We met another investor, a sultan of something or other, who said, "You boys have created something that's going to be a chat universe—a chat of every shape and size." "A chat universe? That's not really what we want to limit the business to," we'd say. But the sultan seemed adamant. He said, "When I give you $100,000, it's going to be a chat universe."

Every time we got a fish on the line, it turned out to be too good to be true or there was a catch. We needed money. We were desperate for money. But at the same time, did we really want investors that would force us into crazy ideas? Once again, we walked away from good money.

Later, we went back to California and met with more angel investors. We met with a guy called Doug Devivo who had founded Aldus Software, and he was willing to put in $100,000. A miracle! We were finding people, but it took an inordinate amount of time. Eventually, by the end of 1996, right as our second-round funds were running out, Cornell suggested we meet with a former alumnus named David Duffield.

Todd and I had just come back from California. We were exhausted. It was freezing. Cornell told us that Duffield ran a large California-based company called PeopleSoft. Todd and I were exhausted from our constant scurrying around. All we'd done was fund-raise. We found it hard to get excited about this meeting and were especially suspicious of an entrepreneur who actually enjoyed visiting Ithaca. But we weren't in a position to turn anyone down.

> > >

So for the umpteenth time, we got in the Corolla. It was snowing. It was foggy. You couldn't even see through the window. We were freezing. We kept our coats on inside the car because the heater didn't work.

We finally arrived at a dive bar, our arranged meeting place in Ithaca. There's David with this look on his face, this spark in his eye as he sees us—two kids—walk in. "God, this is fantastic," he said. "It reminds me of my story. It reminds me of when I had to mortgage my house, and my first few companies failed. But then I created PeopleSoft, guys. Now my net worth is getting close to the billion-dollar mark."

Then he said, "What do you guys intend to raise?"

"We're looking to raise $4 or $5 million," we said, "but we're not getting close to that."

David looked thoughtful for a moment.

Then he said, "Put me down for $200,000 for the second round."

We were so happy, I don't remember getting home that night. By winter 1996, we had closed our third round of financing for nearly $1.2 million (again Duffield was our biggest contributor: This time he put in $500K in our third round of financing). It was short of our preferred goal, yes, but it was still a new lease on life. And it was just enough for us to step up the pace.

Just as we were raising the stakes in the money sweepstakes, theglobe.com was growing as a company. In fact, we'd come a long way. We'd long since discarded our comic strips, and we'd decided to stop mirroring downloadable software from the various sites because that just didn't seem to be a business model.

It may sound obvious now, but we'd just learned that it was all about increasing the number of page views—that was what would generate more ad dollars. So, more chat rooms, more sophisticated technology. We'd launched a home-page builder that let you create custom pages and add graphics. We added a personal ad section, where you could post greetings. (By the way, that feature attracted an almost 90 percent male audience; it was almost embarrassing.)

Our personal ads were actually a turnoff to a lot of VCs. At the time, advertisers were very scared of chat as well. They would go in and see chat room talk about sex and say, "Oh, we don't want to get into that sort of thing." So chat soon became somewhat taboo.

So we focused instead on making the site a more sophisticated and richer community experience. We put more money and effort into beautiful graphics, a nice layout, and navigation assistance. Now you could get around the site easily.

Unfortunately for Todd and me, many of the technological advances came while we were away. Although we were intimately familiar with all aspects of the site and continued to serve as the main proponents for innovation, we found ourselves being increasingly limited in terms of the quality time we could focus on enhancements. As we spent more time looking for money, we had to delegate responsibilities for the first time. Actually, we were forced to learn how to delegate—not a talent you're necessarily born with.

Meanwhile, we still had to finish all our classes. This was just unbearable. We both had a full course load—all day long—right up until the summer of 1996, when we finally graduated by the seat of our pants.

I graduated with roughly a B+ average, but most of the final months of school are a blur. I do remember the commencement ceremony. That afternoon, in front of 5,000 graduating students and 10,000 spectators, Hunter Rawlings, the president of Cornell, interrupted his speech to say, "I'd like to put out a special thanks to Todd Krizelman and Stephan Paternot, who created the largest Macintosh Web site in the world. Congratulations to the two of them."

We had no idea he even knew about us. It turned out that Bob had put in the word to Rawlings. Either way, we felt totally vindicated.

Suddenly, all our fellow students knew what we'd been up to and why we'd disappeared for two years while they were partying. Our teachers finally knew why we'd been missing classes. One of my profs came running up to me and jumped on my back. "I knew you'd been doing something great," she said. We were heroes that day.

After we graduated, we were still running our entire site on Macintosh computers, which is laughable because Macs are hardly made for servers.

Nevertheless, just as Rawlings said, we'd firmly established ourselves as the biggest Mac-based World Wide Web site in the world, generating 14 million hits a month, probably somewhere around a quarter-million monthly users, and Apple had begun to officially use us in their marketing material. That was a big coup. Since we had no money for advertising, it was critical to get press and piggyback on other people's marketing campaigns. Now we were on every Apple brochure. It was us, Target, and Valvoline—a bizarre mix of companies to showcase Apple.

At one point we were even Mac representatives, wearing Apple logoed T-shirts at the Siebold conference in San Francisco, just so we could demonstrate the tools that we'd built to run on Macintosh servers. Any free exposure we could get was worth it. Another such conference presented itself in Austin, Texas, and we were offered free booth space for our company. Todd and I jumped at the occa-

sion and once again headed back to my old favorite state. Not much
of a business plan, but it got us noticed a bit more. On that trip, we
were so broke, we rationed every penny and stayed in a Super 8
Motel.

We may have been attracting some notice in the marketplace, but
we weren't doing much in the personal-life department during the
first few years. Ever since Elayna and I broke up, I'd decided to focus
all my energy on starting this company. By and large, my social life
disappeared. There was no time to travel, no time to bum around, no
time to hang out at the bars, and do all those classic undergrad
things.

Our life in College Town revolved around three stops, all of
which were right beneath our office. A bar called Ruloff's, a Kinko's,
and a Wendy's—the three essential building blocks to any fledgling
business. It was the standard combo no. 1 for $3.51, which consisted
of burger and fries. Then we'd go to Ruloff's for a shot of Jack, and
then to Kinko's to make a few copies. That would be it. That was my
life for two years.

And through it all, Todd and I were together 24 hours a day. It was
getting brutal. That was the real test of our partnership. We had
moved in together, worked together, raised money together, and we
hung out in the same places. Twenty-four hours a day, sitting at the
office, facing each other two feet away. We started to get really
antsy and aggravated and started fighting about little things. It's
almost like a husband-and-wife relationship when stuff between
partners goes bad. We'd have vicious arguments.

Eventually we realized—wait a second—the problem is simple:
We're in each other's faces too often. So after that year, we got separate places. We decided to live our social lives separately, and
voila, our professional relationship flourished. Now we've shared an
office for six years and still get along. We trust each other with our
lives.

Of course, getting our own places didn't ease the burden of working so much in our tiny space. At the office, hygiene essentially went out the window. All I ate was Wendy's. I would speak extra fast. I would walk extra fast. Everything was just hyper speed, hyper everything. That's exactly what it felt like. We could feel the competition of this pioneering new medium; everyone was beginning to notice. We felt this rush. It was a potential new religion.

This was a religion being invented.

Now would come the Crusades.

4

NEW YORK GROOVE

how 3,000 miles in a toyota corolla turned
into $20 million

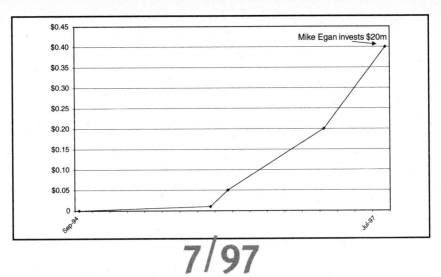

Mike Egan invests $20m

7/97

STOCK PRICE
(private company)

By January 1997, we'd freshly closed our third round of financing with a total of $1.2 million. We thought that would be all the money we'd ever need to reach profitability. And profitability was actually quite close, mainly because our burn rate was superlow. Now there were new decisions to make. Todd and I had just graduated. We had 15 employees. We were still in Ithaca, but I didn't want to spend the rest of my life there.

At the time, Ithaca was desperately trying to retain business. The town was hoping to refashion itself as a bustling metropolis, but frankly, it didn't seem so interested in keeping us. We tried to get help from Cornell, but the university bureaucracy didn't allow it. The businesspeople were just academics, or people who had some vested interest in wanting things to stay the way they were. Some people even seemed insulted by what we were doing. We had really no incentive to stay so we decided it was time to move. And we'd have to move somewhere that was in the middle of the activity.

That meant Boston, New York City, or San Francisco. Everything was in San Francisco at the time. The problem was that neither of us really wanted to go there. Our perception of San Francisco was that it's a one-track town—all engineers. It would have been *Revenge of the Nerds* for the rest of our lives, and I desperately did not want to end up in an engineering mecca like San Francisco.

Besides, if we went to San Francisco, we'd be a tiny fish in a giant pond; we'd be crushed by the competition. There were issues of employee attrition in San Francisco; people there went from one job across the street to another job across the street to yet another job. We'd never be able to hold onto our people. We didn't have the money to retain people. We barely had enough money to advertise and compete.

After ruling out San Francisco, it quickly became clear that we weren't moving to Boston, either. After Cornell, being in a college-oriented town didn't really appeal to either of us.

So, in January 1997, we made the epic decision to move to Manhattan. Guess who was chosen to explore our future location? I headed down to scout it out. The first time I drove to NYC to find an apartment, I was blasting techno music in my Corolla, going faster and faster and faster. Half an hour away from the city, you start seeing the skyline approaching. By the George Washington Bridge, I'd feel the chill of excitement down my spine as I saw the big city arriving. That's how I felt about New York.

Up until then, my impression of Manhattan was based on what I'd heard and seen in the movies. I pictured something straight out of *Highlander*: people running around dark alleyways, whipping out machine guns, sword fights, the whole nine yards. Drug City.

But that's what drew me to New York as well, the threatening element. I got excited by the notion that there would be danger (and opportunity) around every corner. At Cornell, I'd heard all the stories about how you're guaranteed to be mugged within six months of arrival. One of my friends once had a shotgun held to his head at an ATM.

Of course, Giuliani had already sanitized a lot of the city by the time I showed up. After a few days strolling through gentrified neighborhoods, my thought was, *What danger?*

It quickly became apparent to me the ease with which a Manhattanite could meet friends, go out, have a phenomenal time, meet beautiful women. The food was fantastic. All the churning possibilities made me feel as though I'd picked the perfect moment in my life to arrive; I could sort of power up and energize on the blood of the city.

> > >

When I arrived, I didn't know anything about Manhattan. I didn't even understand how the grid system worked. I had no sense of geography. Every time you turn left, everything looks the same: straight streets that go on forever. I tried to find an apartment but didn't know where to begin. So I called up a Realtor right away. He showed me a bunch of pricey apartments I could barely afford. One after the other was a disaster: basement apartments, closets, dumps.

A word about my finances at the time: Todd and I never paid ourselves during the first two and a half years. In fact, when we arrived in New York, we'd just made the radical decision to start paying ourselves $35,000 a year. After taxes, that left me with about $20,000 a year, which after rent. . . .

Simply put, it wasn't enough.

So I arrive in New York. I've got about $4,000 in my bank account (the meager remains from the internship in Texas), and I know it's about to be depleted fast. A few days into my arrival, I made the mistake of leaving my car unattended on a sketchy block for half a day. When I came back, my car was pushed up onto the sidewalk, parked against a fire hydrant, with three or four parking tickets. Meanwhile, someone had decided to deflate my right rear tire. After peeling the tickets off the windshield, I drove around at five miles an hour—*ka-klunk-kaklunk*—to find another parking place. I was completely lost. I drove the car around, found another parking space on another street (not near a fire hydrant), and parked. Over the next 24 hours, I proceeded to find out where to pay off the tickets and plead my case. By the time I came back to the car, all four hubcaps were stolen and my left front mirror was torn off, dangling by a couple of wires. I was lucky when, a few months later, I negotiated its sale for four grand.

I found a little apartment on Sullivan Street, in the Village, between Bleecker Street and West Third. It was 283 square feet, but you couldn't beat that neighborhood. A beautiful 283 square foot apartment for only $1,325 a month. My bedroom was the size of the bed. I couldn't even open and shut the door. The bathroom? You could effortlessly sit on the toilet, stick your feet forward into the shower, and turn on the sink and brush your teeth simultaneously. For the first month while I scouted for an office, I worked in my apartment. I had a tiny desk, one of those square, 1 foot by 1 foot jobs with little flaps, and a little plastic chair. After a few hours of work, I wanted any excuse to get out of my apartment.

Every time I stepped out into the street, I would tell myself, *I'm here. I'm 10,000 miles away from family and friends. I don't know anyone.* Every time I walked on the pavement, I could feel the city's vibe. Car alarms going off, people yelling, motorcycles roaring, students throwing beer bottles in the street, sirens and laughter every few minutes. The noise is what I liked the most because I could shut my eyes and drown out everything else. Most people like to get rid of the noise.

I wanted it.

> > >

I spent the first three months in a mad rush to locate and complete a deal for our office space. Ultimately, I found a loft on Twenty-first Street, a huge raw space, 4,800 square feet, beautiful 18-foot ceilings, and wooden floors. It looked like a total hole when I first arrived. After the team came down, we polished the floor, put in the lights, built up some papier-mâché walls, and made room for 25 people—a huge risk, since we were really living off the month-to-month money we had. At the time, we had about 12 to 15 people in Ithaca, and we knew maybe only 10 of them were coming. But we weren't in a position to overexpand and get a 60-person office. Making room for 25 right out of the gate was a stretch. We debated for quite a while. Then we decided to just hope things worked out well.

When Todd and the staff arrived, the construction team was still building the walls. Literally, the only thing that had been completed was one conference room. So Todd and I put all 10 people in the conference room. We gave ourselves our own little executive office that was maybe 200 square feet.

Because everyone was on top of each other, we all invested in big earphones that were supposed to muffle out noise but instead made us look like helicopter pilots. It didn't help much. After two months, we were ready to kill each other.

Back in Ithaca, our whole site was being run from a few big database machines in one small room. When we moved, a few of the tech guys stayed to run the site. After a couple of months, the time came to bring the server to the big city. So, one weekend morning, we literally took the site off the air while they hauled ass (we put up a notice that said, "We apologize—the site is temporarily down for maintenance"). Six hours later in New York City, we plugged the whole thing back in, wires, everything.

During this period, theglobe.com still had a free service and a subscriber service. This was back in the day when everyone was going free; the concept of subscription hadn't been proven yet to be a failure. For $2.95 a month, you could get yourself private chat rooms, and $4.95 a month got you a silver or gold subscription. For $10 a month, you were platinum, which gave you more home-page storage space.

Then there was the free part of the site. What we realized over the next year or two was that although the subscription service drove decent revenues (something that attracted quite a few investors), it had massively slowed our rate of user growth while everyone else was just rocketing. If we had not done that for those two years while we tried to get it to work, we could have been a Yahoo or a GeoCities in size. But instead, people had to choose between us or a free service, and a lot of them went somewhere else. In hindsight, that had been one of our bad, bad early moves with subscriptions. But whatever. At least we had the experience, and we learned from it. That was part of the service, and in fact, that's what I think really attracted Michael Egan (our soon-to-be new chairman). Michael came in with these visions of creating tens of thousands of communities, each with 10 members, each paying $10 a month, and if we all did it, it would work out to billions of dollars in revenue.

By May, after what seemed an eternity, the construction was completed. Everyone got their own cubes: the classic communal office space of the Internet start-up age. This was the big time. We were in New York City. Everyone was excited. Some were scared. They didn't know what to do in New York or where to go. As a four-month vet, I was dishing out suggestions to all the employees, showing all the restaurants and the different things to do.

At the time, New York was trying to attract business. Giuliani had set up an economic development program, trying to attract and retain businesses. From that, we got our first major press: a tiny mention about our arrival in the *New York Times*. The article said something like, "IBM moves 10,000 employees to New York City, and WebGenesis sets up office in New York City." (We'd officially changed our name to theglobe.com, but people still kept calling us WebGenesis.) "Mentioned in the same breath with IBM!" Todd and I groaned. "Everyone is going to think we're a multitrillion-dollar company now."

At the time, there was still no such thing as Silicon Alley. There were a few Web shops, but none had the sophistication of the major companies found in San Francisco. The first snippets of what would come to be defined as the new economy were coming out—you heard about people working around the clock, sleeping under their desks, things like that. We had been living it, too. It wasn't unusual to find Todd and me in the office at 2:00 in the morning, watching the servers, rebooting the ones that kept crashing. But we loved it. It was a fever.

Although we'd been briefly profitable the preceding year, we knew the expense of setting up in New York City would put us back in the red. Nevertheless, our traffic kept climbing. Ad sales kept climbing. We really didn't have much of an in-house sales force, but we'd made some hires to do marketing and sales. Todd and I were set to return to profitability by that fall. All it would take was $100,000 a month. (Shortly after Michael invested, Todd and I came to the conclusion that the only way we could compete was in scale.) It became clear that we couldn't get anyone to pay for the service. Sure, we had some 30,000 paying subscribers, but that would only earn us $100,000 to $200,000 a month in revenue—hardly the big advertising dollars. Soon thereafter, we scrapped the subscription business model. As soon as we did, our traffic rocketed out of control to the point where our servers exploded. I mean, they were melting. We couldn't even keep them up any more. At the time, it was more important, if you will, to be a big mighty television network with big-money ads than to be a small for-pay Discovery Channel. There was much more glamour and power to advertising revenue, and we were all attracted to that.

Sometime in mid-March, I got a call from Hunter Rawlings, and everything changed. Rawlings said, "Hey, boys. I'm down in Florida meeting with an alumnus. Name is Michael Egan. He runs this car company, Alamo Rent-A-Car. Turns out the guy's looking for the next great hurrah. He wants to get into the media business, and I thought I had the two perfect guys for him to meet."

We looked at each other, "Oh, God, the car business? Another flake from Florida? What the hell is this?" Needless to say, we were very skeptical. Rawlings wouldn't hear it. He said, "The guy wants to meet with you. He's flying up to Ithaca."

Todd and I had vowed to *never* return. Now there we were, flying to Ithaca, depressed out of our minds. But when we arrived, we saw Mike disembark from his private jet.

Out rolled the red carpet. Then came the entourage. *My God,* we thought, *this guy has a private jet! This is for real.* That day Mike's entourage included Ed Cespedes, formerly from JP Morgan and Mike's new mergers & acquisitions (M&A) guru; Rosalie Arthur, Mike's chief accountant; and several others. Todd and I were with Rawlings.

Hunter decided to let us meet at Statler Hall on campus. We had this huge lunch behind private doors; everything was shut down around us.

Now why, you ask, was a guy like Michael Egan interested in a couple of twentysomething kids? At the time, Mike had just sold Alamo Rent-A-Car for $625 million to Wayne Huizenga's Auto-Nation, which allowed him to get into the M&A business. Michael's net worth had gone up to about $1 billion (though mostly in stock). Ed had left JP Morgan to help start Dancing Bear Investments, Michael's new angel investor group in Fort Lauderdale, Florida. Ed had essentially negotiated the whole Alamo deal, while managing Mike's personal finances; he was considered an M&A whiz kid, and he was only in his early thirties.

So we had our meeting. As usual, Todd and I laid on the community rap. It was all about community (it was still a fairly pioneering concept in those days). We'd become pretty good at our pitch.

By then, Todd and I were intimately familiar with the community business. We now used the phrase *media play.* We knew about the evolution of the advertising market. We knew the online social dynamics—what worked and what didn't—right down to the kinds of icons that people preferred. We also had the confidence of knowing that we'd progressively raised more and more money each year. Up to this point we'd probably raised close to $2 million. At the time, we were 23 years old, and people were still taken aback by how baby-faced we were, which only forced us to improve our pitch. We could literally finish each other's sentences, machine-gun style. We could take anybody.

At the end of the meeting, Mike said, "Well, I want in."

Mike was a big guy, vaguely reminiscent of Leslie Nielsen (think *Naked Gun*), only larger, with a friendly face, baby blue eyes, and white hair. Despite his size, he was never wearing less than an impeccably tailored suit. We were struck by Mike's tremendously engaging, enthusiastic persona.

The air seemed to be sucked out of the room after he spoke. There was a pause. Then he added, "I'm ready to put in $5 million."

Todd and I looked at each other. A few months earlier, we would have been screaming. Now we felt ambivalent, like *hold on just a second here*. We'd just raised $1.2 million. We didn't critically need that much money right now. We didn't want an investor with some hugely disparate agenda co-running our show. We felt really unsure about the offer.

But.

On the other hand, this could be the money that would finally open our door into the big leagues. Remember, everyone in San Francisco had been raising $10, $15, even $20 million. This could be our chance to catch up.

We agreed to the offer but made it clear that Todd and I would run the company. This was our venture, and we wanted to grow with it. We were doing it because we loved the business.

As we spoke, Mike got this childish look in his eyes. He seemed like one of those rare people who could really understand what

Todd and I were talking about. As soon as we finished, he looked like he wanted to take it to the next level. You could tell that he had this exciting dreamer quality about him. His entrepreneurial vision was obvious. It was boring holes through the walls, inventing possibility out of anything it wanted to.

Beyond Alamo, Mike was one of the main investors who'd helped start Nantucket Nectars, which had taken huge market share away from Snapple and Ocean Spray and become a $100 million business. He had won the Horatio Alger award, and it became very clear that whatever Mike touched turned to gold.

I should mention that our style of dress still hadn't changed much. In fact, what did quickly change were Mike's clothes. He went from wearing a suit, which he had done his whole life, to wearing nothing but black. It made him look more up-to-date, and for a 56-year-old guy venturing into uncharted territory, that was key. Mike jumped into the Internet with a great intensity. It was inspiring to witness someone well into middle-age changing his lifestyle and his mentality.

> > >

Lunch ended five hours later. Not only were we ambivalent about Mike's $5 million offer, we were also convinced that either we wouldn't hear back from him or he'd call and change the terms. We'd certainly learned our lesson after all those rounds of financing— things never work out the way you hope.

As we suspected, despite Michael's enthusiasm, the negotiations dragged through April, May, June, July, and August of 1997—five months. The process represented far more due diligence and painful negotiations than we'd ever endured with any VC firm or investors or anyone. This was the biggest drilling ever, and in the end, it turned out to be fantastic. Todd and I became more intimately familiar with the details of our business than ever before, modeling out all the numbers, the projections, everything. We had to bust our asses to get all this stuff worked out. We'd negotiate, negotiate, negotiate.

Mike had his law firm in Florida; we had ours in California. We were constantly negotiating back and forth. The difficulty was that Michael used a more conservative firm whereas ours was high-flying and technology-driven. The principles of how things worked—stock options, contracts, noncompete clauses—were all so different. In California, noncompetes are taken much more lightly; in New York they're taken very seriously and are enforced. Michael wanted to negotiate these stringent, noncompetes that basically stipulated that if Todd and I ever left theglobe.com we could never even contemplate working in the technology or computer field at large. It was just ridiculous! That part of the negotiation took a great deal of time but in the end was resolved to everyone's satisfaction.

Through it all, Todd and I were flying to California constantly. Every time we thought we were almost closing, it kept getting delayed and delayed. This was the time, by the way, when our own personal debt started piling up in anticipation of the deal. We'd been spending our own money and ramped up our company burn rate. It wasn't massive, but we'd gone from $100,000 a month to $150,000 a month. The problem was, at this rate, our $1.2 million was going to run out. Actually, it was imminent. We had $1.2 million in January. Ten months later, we were down to our last few dollars.

Headaches. Gnawed fingernails. Sleeplessness. One afternoon, as I was walking home, I just started trembling with the realization that we were either on the verge of death or the verge of massive success. It was tearing me apart. I began getting massive stomachaches to the point where I was in great pain. Sitting at my desk, I could not handle the pain. It was this uncontrollable acidic discomfort, as if I'd been shot in the stomach, and it didn't matter what I ate. I got the pain before I ate; I got the pain after I ate. I tried eating just salads, but the pain was still there. I had checkups, blood tests, and nothing ever showed up. Finally, the doctor told me that there was only one test left, involving a camera and a truly invasive procedure. I decided to pass on that.

Then I noticed that what had ostensibly happened was my phys-iognomy changed. I had become lactose intolerant and allergic to a dozen other things. I eventually discovered that when you undergo astronomical levels of stress, your body can change. You can be-come allergic to something that never bothered you before. I'd always been healthy, but all of a sudden, God gave me a thousand-pound bag of sand. Eventually, I learned to control it, but during those five months of negotiations, Mike wasn't making digestion any easier.

Over the course of our meetings, Mike made it clear to us that he wanted to own at least 50 percent of theglobe.com. And Michael played hardball. He said, "I'm going to value your business at $10 million, and if I want 50 percent, that means I'm going to put in $10 million." By his calculations, he'd own $10 million of a $20 million business postfinancing.

Meanwhile, our board was enthusiastic, "Guys, if you can get $5 million, let alone $10 million, that would be a miracle. Don't push it." But Todd and I still believed we were worth more. I remember sitting down with Mike and saying, "Mike, I feel like you're really lowballing us. I really feel like this business is worth (okay here we go, fingers crossed) $40 million." Now, for an Internet company, especially after what I'd seen Yahoo, Lycos, and all those companies go for, this was perfectly reasonable. In fact, I thought we were worth *more*.

Then Michael said, "Look, guys. I don't mean to lowball you. I'll need to talk to Ed and my staff about this." They actually went to another room to do so. Sitting in silence, Todd got that look that said, *If we pull this off, Steph, I'm really going to love you. But if we don't. . . . !* It was like poker. The minute we looked nervous was the minute they'd know they had us.

They came back from the board meeting, and we regrouped around the table. Michael was going to put in $20 million instead of the original $5 million.

Oh, my God. We had danced with the devil in the pale moonlight. All kinds of crazy things like that started going through my mind. Of course, we'd find out later that Egan had been wildly hesitant. It was a lot of money. He'd never made an investment that big (*no one* had ever made an investment that big in the industry).

On top of that, Egan was used to traditional businesses, the old multiple to profit thing. It is stating the obvious today, but in the context of Internet companies, standard methods of valuation simply didn't apply. It was thrilling, untrammeled terrain for Egan (and anybody else) who was trying to figure out what an Internet site was worth in 1997. It was also practically impossible. Rosalie, being a conservative accountant, was dead set against a deal at this price. Fortunately, Ed sat down with him to do comparative analysis, after which he said, "Look, Todd and Steph are right. There are valuations out there that set a precedent for this. Despite the risk, this could be the biggest thing you've ever done in your life." He wrote this in a memo that recommended moving forward.

As a reward for his influence with Mike, Ed came to New York City and spent the next five months with us. He'd just relocated his entire life to Florida, including his fiancée. For the first time, it wasn't Todd and me who had to keep the process going. Now Ed was pushing it and challenging us to keep up with him, until we working 24 hours a day, falling asleep at odd hours at our desks and waking up surrounded by stacks of half empty cartons of Chinese food. Internet mania felt like the Indianapolis 500: fast and furious.

Among the first things that had to be negotiated were our contracts—Todd and I never had one. We had just started making $35,000 a year. We looked at each other practically in a trance, "What an opportunity, what should we ask for? Should we ask for, I don't know, like $100,000?" That seemed like an outlandish number. Of course, CEOs of any traditional company were making far more than that. But could we really dare start there? What if that was too much, and they decided to walk away from the deal? Did we want to take this risk? Maybe it would be better to take the money from the investment and ask for $40,000. We decided to live large.

So we sat down with Ed. "Ed," I said with the deepest voice I could muster, "Todd and I would like to do $100,000 each."

And Ed said, "Guys, let's just call it $125,000 each."

We were taken aback. "What? You just made it more? Done!" This time the poker faces slipped. When you have enough bad experiences, you learn to accept when something seems to have gone well. (Ed, we subsequently discovered, is a stellar negotiator. Not only is he brilliant financially, his power play is that he knows how to befriend the people he's negotiating with. He makes himself much more than a go-between. In other words, you end up feeling like he's giving you the inside scoop from the other team, even though he's the negotiator for the acquiring party.)

Naturally, $125,000 each made us feel very comfortable, but the reality is that Todd and I never wanted to sell our business. We never wanted to give up control on anything. But he alone persuaded us. Ed said, "Mike's only doing this if you guys stay as CEOs, if you guys commit to a 10-year contract." Then we'd negotiate more. Ultimately, we got it down to a five-year contract, which was two or three years more than anyone else had been signing in California. Again, to make us feel smart, there was a kicker. In addition to the $125,000 each, and to soften the five-year commitment and the loss of autonomy, Mike was going to give us $500,000—in cash—each. This, as they well knew, was something we just couldn't refuse. Todd and I were broke, our bank accounts were down to zero, and we had accumulated large debts. Of course, then we discovered the U.S. tax law, and 50 percent of it was already gone. Nevertheless, the net $250,000 seemed to us to be a new lease on life. All of a sudden, everything we'd worked for wasn't evaporating. Finally, I could hold my head up to my Cornell buddies who were already making $200,000 or $300,000 a year at Goldman Sachs. Mike gave us the first chance to get out of our crappy rentals and actually buy real apartments, which is where I live now. How were we to know that it would be the biggest fortune we'd ever accumulate? But I was lucky; I knew I could live off this money for a while.

> > >

When the deal finally seemed to be happening, Todd and I flew yet again to California. We decided we were going to sit at the table of our law firm and stay there until the deal was done.

Finally, after 36 straight hours, the deal terms came in, we exchanged documents, and we signed. Todd and I hopped back on the red-eye, flew to New York, arrived first thing in the morning, went to the office, and shut our door. Todd conked out on a futon. I was lying on the floor. We just passed out for an hour.

When we woke up, we realized that it was done—$20 million in the bank! Then, we checked with our bank and confirmed that the money had been wired in. It was a done deal. We called a meeting with our staff. They had no clue what was going on. Some of them had speculated that because we'd been gone so much, we were selling the company. When we announced that we'd just closed $20 million, everyone's jaws just dropped.

Within a few days, we ended up in the *New York Times*. There was a front-page story in the Metro section. You couldn't miss it. There was a picture of Todd and me—me still with my stupid ponytail. (My hair, by the way, had grown longer and longer. Later, in the fall of 1997, my sister came to visit and talked me into shaving it all off.) The picture was from the computer conference in Texas. The headline read, "Whiz Kids Land $20 Million for Their Chat Room." It was labeled the biggest investment in history by an individual. Thus began a huge wave of press. Suddenly, the West Coast took notice. Until then, the West Coast had a serious superiority complex—it was still the classic *Revenge of the Nerds*. Anything outside was considered inferior. For them, it was as though they were the engineering town, the smart guys, and everyone else was cow dung. (In some cases it was justified, the New York Internet world was, for some time, mainly an artsy-fartsy scene, an opportunity for people to dye their hair, don thick-rimmed glasses, and tote around little portable iBooks.) We suddenly were a big fish in an even bigger, more deluxe pond, and certainly the leading player in New York. We had $20 million, and more important, we had secured the mezzanine round of financing needed for an IPO.

The IPO was the final stage, the ultimate right of passage. It was the stamp of approval that proved this is not just hype, there's actual money to be made here. Being public meant you were legit. It meant that you'd attract more advertisers, and it made it easier to attract more money and employees. Suddenly, we could envision that TGLO symbol moving across the ticker—just like we'd seen with Yahoo, whose revenues ballooned after they went public. The dream was to do it in under 18 months.

Twelve months later, we went public.

5

MICHAEL EGAN AND THE ROAD TO THE IPO

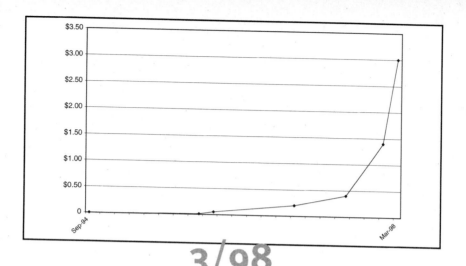

STOCK PRICE
(private company)

We got the $20 million financing on August 13, 1997, and the events of the following few months happened very fast. For one thing, this quickly marked the getting-to-know-the-new-partner period. Egan was so proud of his new investment that he built his entire office shaped like a globe: He made a circular space with a conference room and super hi-tech monitors connected to computers. All his furniture was circular.

Unbeknownst to us, Michael already had visions for theglobe .com. He'd been simultaneously working on other little investments, things he was interested in folding into our company. Among the first of many companies we'd hear about from Egan was something called IntelliTravel, a network of 70,000 travel agents.

IntelliTravel was Egan's multilevel online travel marketing concept. It was run by guys who always seemed to be sporting slicked-back hair and perennial tans. The main guy seemed to ooze money and didn't appear to have nearly enough time to spend his newfound wealth. When Egan introduced him to Todd and me, our initial reaction was, "What in God's name are we doing with these guys?" But Egan had this concept. He'd experienced great success in the travel business. Now he wanted to combine IntelliTravel with theglobe.com and sell it online. "You guys could have this huge revenue stream underneath." At first, Todd and I thought it sounded like it had potential. We'd instantly have thousands more salespeople who weren't even on our payroll.

Then we realized Michael was saying we'd also be instantly responsible for the entire travel company, and that was intimidating. But Egan was extremely persuasive, "We could have 70,000 travel priests preaching about theglobe.com." Priests?

Egan couldn't contain his enthusiasm. "Imagine," he said, "70,000 people! All of them able to make a little bit of money if they're able to sell subscriptions for theglobe.com." Egan was presaging AOL selling Time-Warner subscriptions by wanting his IntelliTravel agents to sell $5-a-month subscriptions to theglobe.com on top of their travel packages. It certainly sounded interesting. At least it did until we actually met the team. These guys were like bottled L.A. oil. Working together would have been the most lethal combination. They wore such crisp suits you could hear them coming by the swoosh of their pants.

We talked Michael out of merging with IntelliTravel, but every month or so, he wanted to have a management meeting in which he'd bring together the heads of all his different investments. After IntelliTravel, there was New River Technology, a little firm that helped do tech for his travel company. Every time we went down to his office in Fort Lauderdale, Egan would sit at the end of this long table and the rest of us would join him. Though he'd made it clear to his staff that theglobe.com was his crown jewel, it seemed from our perspective that Egan was trying to combine his companies with ours in some advantageous way. We wanted to get busy preparing theglobe.com to go public and keep growing the thing. We considered these potential deals with a grain of salt.

At one point, Egan basically told us, "Guys, we've got to get this working better. We're losing money." He just started slapping the table. "Show me the money. Guys, *show me the money!*" It was right after *Jerry McGuire* had come out, and this expression was getting overused fast.

Through it all, Egan never really yelled at Todd and me; apparently, we were always "the boys." He didn't want to scare us off, and at the same time we believed that his only hope in hell of having anything to do with the Internet was keeping on board the two young guys who really lived and breathed this medium. It was difficult—Michael wanted total accountability for everything. But this was back before statistics were standardized (actually, they're still not standardized). It was so hard to measure everything.

Even with our traffic—now over the million-user mark—there were always questions as to performance. Fluctuations would be hard to explain. You would think your numbers were going up, then you'd reprocess your logs, and they had gone down. We spent a lot of time explaining to Mike and others that this business was hard to measure because there were very few standards.

By February, Egan backed off a bit and we postponed the meetings. He stopped forcing us down to Florida. Somehow, Ed had suggested to Egan that for theglobe.com to grow, he had to let it really run. Egan responded by sending Ed to New York. (We'd started talking about the IPO and what we could do to get there within 18 months.) At the time, Ed was 32. This was at the beginning of 1998, so I would have just been turning 24. Having Ed in the city was fantastic. We had a great time. He was a former banker and could speak banker lingo. He knew everybody and has access to bankers that Todd and I couldn't get to. With Ed in place, we started the IPO process in earnest.

Still, it wasn't easy getting the bankers on board. We had a tough time getting a response because there was no IPO or Internet mania—yet. Bankers were doing their usual deals. The big bulge brackets guys—the Merrill Lynches, the Goldman Sachs, Morgan Stanley—were backlogged with their traditional IPOs: Fox, all these major telcos, things like that. They had no real Internet analysts, no Internet divisions, no Internet focus at all. Merrill Lynch, for instance, had zero Internet focus (their CEO would get beaten up in the press for not having any Internet strategy when this stuff hit).

In addition to fighting for financial attention, we were working simultaneously on the preparation of a major ad campaign. One of the most notable things Todd and I discovered the preceding year was that all these new sites who were competing with us for the same audience had launched their first television ad campaigns. Excite had launched the "Are you experienced?" campaign; Yahoo had the goofy fishermen pulling a giant bass out of a pond after having searched for bait. The visibility of the competitors had really picked up. To keep competing in the big leagues, we needed to create greater visibility for our brand.

We'd been preparing for this since the month after Mike's investment closed, and we'd been meeting a lot of different agencies, trying to figure out who could come up with the right campaign for us. We ended up choosing Kirshenbaum, who ultimately developed an amazing campaign for theglobe.com. The tag line was "A Whole New Life Awaits You" in neon-green text on black. There was a reason we picked those colors. Doubleclick had proven that neon-green on black provided a 17 percent higher click-through rate on banner ads. For the first time, you were able to measure the effectiveness of a color. Neon-green it was.

We decided to spend $8 million on a massive campaign—$8 million out of the $20 million we had. It seems ludicrous now, but back then, investor mentality had gone through a major evolution. We were just entering the phase when investors had gone from getting excited about pure concepts to believing that the site's traffic determined which company was the biggest and the best. At the beginning of 1998, losses were irrelevant. That was the key thing. Losses were irrelevant, and growth rate was *everything*. Coined by Netscape, the industry's operating expression was GBF, "Get big fast," and it was quickly used by everybody. We were looking ahead to an IPO and the dream of a lot more money. Even one of our board members said, "Guys, spend your $20 million as if you had $40 million. Ramp up, that's what matters right now." We agreed. "We'll take the $8 million and really advertise the bejesus out of this site."

Kirshenbaum developed an incredible ad campaign for television. We had several different commercials, but they were all very ethereal. In one, there was a black background and our logo would come rotating in this sphere out of nowhere. There were futuristic pulsating lights, and this sexy British female voice that said, "Is this the Age of Aquarius? If so, you could meet your partner online." The voice would say, "theglobe.com offers chat, home-page building. . . ." We played up all our novel concepts.

We launched nationwide—on cable channels, MTV, networks, the whole nine yards. We were the first online community to do any type of advertising and the fourth or fifth site to launch a TV ad campaign. We saturated the New York market. Buses said, "A Whole New Life Awaits You." We had billboards, all strategically placed in front of other ad agencies, so they would know where to advertise. We tried to hit all the demographics. We wanted the site to appeal to everybody. But the MTV crowd—those responsive twentysomethings—became our best market.

People started recognizing our logo. Todd and I would walk down the street in theglobe.com T-shirts. We'd get stopped, "Hey, what is that logo? I recognize it from TV. What is theglobe.com? What's it about?" There's nothing so strangely exciting as having people in the street recognize your logo. At that point, the bankers started getting a lot more responsive. Suddenly, they were thinking that theglobe.com is the next big thing. This community stuff is amazing. And community did make us different from what GeoCities and these other places were offering. They were really home-page–based sites. Our philosophy was more about people interacting with other people. Very quickly, everyone started using the term *community*. Everyone jumped on the bandwagon. Everyone *became* community.

The hype was building, the bankers started showing interest, and two of the smaller but more aggressive banks came right after us—Bear Stearns and Volpe Brown. Now, at this point we had expanded to a staff of maybe 60 people. We had completely saturated our floor; 60 people in a space for 25. It was a rat maze, little *Matrix* cubicles everywhere. Volpe Brown is a West Coast boutique firm. They came into our little conference room that has such thin walls that you could hear the nearby elevator clinking up and down. Todd, Ed, and I walked them through theglobe.com story.

A few days later, the Bear Stearns team, who were always impeccably dressed in suits, came down to pitch us on why *they* would be the right player. Todd and I appeared in dramatic contrast to them, dressed in some completely schlubby outfits. I had just cut my hair, going from my college ponytail to a short messy style. Those bankers must have looked at us and thought, *Oh, yes. Young Internet kids*. They tried to relax with us, but it was so transparent. There would always be the standard small talk at the beginning of the meeting, all this stilted banter about clothing and clubs. Bankers versus Internet guys; a classic standoff for the late nineties.

We met with other banks as well, including Mary Meeker at Morgan Stanley and Michael Parekh at Goldman Sachs. It turned out that Goldman was going to take GeoCities public. GeoCities, a company founded by David Bohnett in L.A., was the largest home-page–hosting site in the world and on a run rate to generate twice our revenue. In 1997, our biggest problem was that we'd generated under $1 million in revenues, and we were on a run rate in 1998 to generate $5 million in revenues. These bankers typically wouldn't work with a company that only did $5 million in revenue and had massive losses. Our understanding was that the minimum they like to touch are companies with $10 million in revenues annually and climbing. It was hard for them. We met with a great banker at Merrill Lynch who loved us and wanted to take us public and to think out of the box. But again, we didn't meet all of the required criteria and their analysts refused to budge their decision until we'd hit that revenue benchmark. We couldn't wait.

Timing was everything; Todd and I could feel the market literally heating up. We had to be the first in the community space. Second was okay. But no one ever remembers who's third, and the rest are completely off the map. This became apparent with search engines. It was common knowledge. If GeoCities was going with Goldman, we'd have to race to get ahead, and if we couldn't get ahead of them, we'd have to be second—or else.

Now, we'd heard disturbing things about some of the big investment banks. Imagine two little seals swimming up to a great white shark and kissing the tip of his nose. That's how we felt, giving ourselves to one of these institutions. But we didn't have much of a choice. And Bear Stearns was being the most aggressive—something that others warned could be off-putting. Still, they were willing to push us, as they did with other Internet companies, when all these other guys wouldn't.

> > >

So we signed on with Bear Stearns and Volpe Brown, and—immediately—the process began. Between April and the end of July, a four-month period, we worked nonstop. Todd and I were barely in the office anymore. We set up a war room down at our law firm at Fried Frank, which was in the financial district, and spent every single day there with all of our bankers, plus all of Bear Stearns' bankers.

This was the other really tough part. We didn't have a chief financial officer (CFO) or a chief operating officer (COO) yet. We were just a bunch of Internet guys, so a part of the deal was that we had to appoint a senior management team immediately in order to go public. We couldn't even file our S1 unless we had this team in place. So the hunt was on simultaneously to find a good CFO. We hired a head-hunting agency, but couldn't find anyone with the appropriate fit.

Then Frank Joyce walked in. Frank boasted a media background. He had been at the Reed Travel Group, which had $300 million in revenue and 2,500 employees. So we negotiated his deal and injected him right into the filing process, where he'd be interacting with the bankers. He had to walk in, accept the financial model that we had developed, refine it with us, and jump right into the pit of fire, which he did from Day One.

We'd also been looking to hire a senior director of business development. We hadn't really thought about a COO before, but we wanted a senior manager with expertise to help us run the daily business. This search was a disaster until the night we met Dean Daniels. Dean had worked in network television at CBS for his entire career. He'd been one of their top guys and was even nominated for four Emmy awards for a piece he'd done on Clinton's infamous "I never inhaled" speech. At first, we weren't even sure that he was the right person for us considering his pure television background, but everything he said was music to our ears. "Guys," he said, "I've been working in the television business. When something goes down on the air, you have three seconds to fix it." We knew right away that he was the kind of hands-on business pro that we needed, and right before our final SEC filing, he came on board.

This, by the way, was the first time we'd hired executives who were quite a bit older than us (both in their forties), and we knew this could be awkward. Our ages had been an issue when we were raising money, so we'd made it clear that we were looking for a more experienced CFO and COO who could essentially help us build the company and lend their management expertise to the business. Our experience was limited to the four years of running the company, and we were missing some of the skills associated with managing a public company. We needed the best help we could get.

And we did need help. As we got closer to the filing process, it felt like we were forming our own ice bridge to skate along. Our entire team always felt on the edge. The reality is that IPOs are a rarity, and few CEOs experience them throughout their entire careers. We were learning everything in real time. Questions kept popping into our heads that would never concern more experienced CEOs. What exactly is a red herring? Why does the SEC have a 30-day wait period? As soon as we'd learn something, we had to instantly assume the demeanor of executives who had being doing this for a long time. It was like our brains were just running on a billion cycles a second. Todd and I had always internalized business moves and focused on the technological and operational details, down to the last megabyte. For example, every home page had to be done just right. Ultimately, that was good for the business because we'd developed good eyes. But at the same time, I'm sure our team wanted to shoot us because we micromanaged the hell out of them.

> > >

If we had to step up to the plate and start making bigger strategic decisions, life at the office wasn't making things any easier. We knew that if we went public we would have to think about pursuing acquisitions, managing financing issues, and meeting other CEOs. We'd need a lot more time doing external things. It was time to delegate and trust that our executive team could do the job.

That was easier said than done. Every week there was some sort of mini crisis. Take our server room. We didn't have the wisdom to think anything through, so the room had been overpacked and installing air-conditioning was an afterthought. So we put in cheap, cooling systems that started spraying water on the computers, which was not only bad for the servers but life-threatening for the staff since there was wiring all over the place. At one point, we consumed so much electricity the meter melted and everything shut down. The meter, by the way, was located right next to our only emergency exit, and there were phone lines and other wires everywhere. It was just hazardous. Our best solution for fixing the electricity meter was to take a broom and jam it in there, which kept the switch up and prevented the thing from flipping off. The problem was the broom would slip and fall right across the fire exit. Naturally, there were some complaints.

We also had our share of human resource problems. In the market climate that was a young Silicon Alley, we employed a few people who really had a little *too much* job experience. One person in particular, an important hire for business development, seemed to have held as many jobs as years she had lived. And it was no surprise: She was a screaming, threatening, empire-builder. After a brief honeymoon in which she established her place in the company, she proceeded to terrorize us with intraoffice power plays. There would be days when she would walk down to our office and just scream obscenities and react to what she apparently perceived as attempts to undermine her authority. It rarely gets more overt than that.

Todd and I were reluctant to dismiss her since we depended on her position for so much (not to mention how many people she was in charge of and how many she had persuaded into her corner). This, of course, is a standard problem that anyone would experience but typically doesn't have a contingency plan for. She bullied us like middle school kids simply because we were young founders.

Then we hired Dean, and his first order of business was to help us with the situation. That same day, we convinced her to resign.

While all of this was going on, we were going to the law firm, day in and day out. Every day, there'd be 15 people in the room with bankers and lawyers on both sides, dug into the conference room trenches filled with bagels, sandwiches, chips, fruit, cookies, and expensive suits. Our teams, our lawyers; their team, their lawyers. We would go in there at 8:00 A.M., start working, have lunch, keep working, go home at 9:00 P.M., shower and go back in until 3 A.M. the next morning. Round the clock, including Saturdays when our friends and coworkers were out partying, Todd and I kept the pressure up. We could have gone slower, but the reality was we had to catch up to GeoCities.

Then we found out that a new company called Xoom.com (a company run by Laurent Massa, who we later became friends with) was going public at the same time we were. Of course, Xoom.com was an e-commerce company camouflaged as a community site in order to take advantage of the community hype. And who was taking them public? Bear Stearns, our very same bankers.

Todd and I had always been overly cautious in general, fearful of others finding out what we were doing and fearful of competitors. Maybe 20 to 30 years of experience makes you more comfortable with competition so that you don't panic as much, but Andy Grove's theory of "Only the Paranoid Survive" clearly applied to us. And paranoia manifests itself in terms of always looking out for the dark horse. Who is it you don't know about that's going to pop out of nowhere? We were well aware of GeoCities. But Xoom was an unknown, and their reach seemed to be ballooning. Now, to our horror, Bear Stearns was working with them as well, which was our worst nightmare. We could easily end up being third to the market . . . and we all knew what people thought about who comes in third. Despite all assurances from our banker that we were a strong player in this sector, we remained nervous about Xoom's representation.

Now, Ed is a big tough guy, he's the kind of guy who knows how to intimidate bankers. But our investment banker assured him there was nothing to worry about, that there was a Chinese wall that couldn't be broken. Nevertheless, we were skeptical. How could we not be with so much riding on the IPO?

> > >

Meanwhile, month after month, as Todd and I worked on our financial model, we learned more about valuation. Around this time, GeoCities went public. They were valued at $250 million, and their market cap rocketed to $1.5 billion. We thought this was phenomenal. They were trading at a multiple of 13. Everything was based on multiples of revenue for the following year. So we tried to calculate what our next year's revenue would be. We projected as being $15, $16, $17, $18 million—a multiple of that. That's the way we valued everything—by looking at the average of the players trading at the time. Nowadays, of course, things have completely changed.

So, that's where GeoCities was trading, and that's what we were trying to get to. Actually, we wanted our market cap to be even higher. Mike wanted it higher. I wanted it higher. Everyone wanted it higher. The only way to make our market cap higher was to come out and say, "All right then, revenues will be higher." It just meant we had to push our revenues. The side effect of this insanity, naturally, was that Todd and I were starting to get really nervous. We'd meet with the board and say, "Um, guys, we've pushed our revenues projections to nearly unrealistic heights. Todd and I will have to kill ourselves to make these numbers." (Turns out we nearly did kill ourselves yet managed to beat earnings every single quarter for the first two years.)

But there was just too much momentum. The thought was to project that we're worth $130 million, so when we filed to go public, we'll be worth $130 million. Bear Stearns decided to price our deal at $11 to $13 a share. For the 10 to 11 million outstanding shares of the company, that would value us at about $130 million, and our offering would be about 3 million shares, which meant we could raise anywhere between $33 and $40 million in cash, which would be just perfect. We thought we were ready to file . . . until the latest debacle.

> > >

In a surprise move, Mike came to us with a proposition: "Guys, I'd like to be CEO, too." This was the first time Todd and I heard of this idea. We spoke with Bob who was always there to support us. Fortunately, he went to Mike and said, "It's tough enough having two CEOs, but it's not unheard of. Three CEOs is a nonstarter. When someone comes calling, when an investor comes calling with questions, you can't have three different answers."

Michael backed down, and we filed the whole document on July 24. We celebrated like wild because the minute you file, the press knows instantly, and the story goes out. Suddenly, theglobe.com was a high-visibility player, and our timing looked good. NASDAQ was absolutely at its peak. It had reached something like 2,500 points. The press was going crazy, and Todd and I finally took a deep sigh. We knew the real work was ahead. Right away, we'd have to start practicing, training for the IPO and the inevitable road show that would commence in September. We'd have one month to six weeks preparation, max. Todd and I wanted desperately to take some time off. I don't think we'd had a single day of vacation since Cornell. Before the road show, we officially had 80 employees, and we'd been in New York for a year and a half. We had 5 or 6 million monthly users.

We never got that vacation. Unbeknownst to us then, the NASDAQ would begin to fall the following week. In fact, we had the misfortune of beginning our road show on one of the single biggest point drops in NASDAQ history.

But, as they say, the show must go on.

6
NEW YORK, NEW YORK
a brave new world

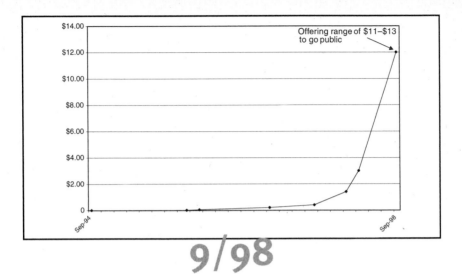

9/98

STOCK PRICE
(private company)

During the first three quarters of 1997, I was living on $35,000 a year. I was netting $2,000 a month; $1,325 of that went to rent. I had less than $665 a month for spending money, about $600 of which would go to food. I still had the original $4,000 in my bank account, but that started shrinking by about $1,000 a month.

So when Mike invested and my salary became $125,000, I could start living. And I did, because suddenly I had more money than I knew what to do with. I could actually afford to go out, I could afford to spend money at the same rate as my friends who'd gone to Goldman or Merrill or law firms.

> > >

Remember, I was a 24-year-old foreigner who'd just moved to Manhattan, and I'd been working like a dog nonstop. I just wanted to get out and pound the pavement. I had a few friends from Cornell who were also in the city, and we started going out regularly. I'd leave the office and head straight out for dinner around 9:30 or 10:00 (as opposed to Cornell when everyone dined at 6:00). I quickly realized how international Manhattan could feel, a city of countless cultures smashed together and mixing on a tiny island. I used to frequent this restaurant called Diva, down in Soho, which I remember both for their open windows and their stunning hostesses.

My friends and I would sit at the bar for half an hour, knock back a few drinks, and by midnight, we'd finish eating. The classic thing was to head over to 23 Watt Street, to a club called Chaos. Chaos was an incredible club with plush red velvet, dark colors, red lights, and people in black clothing. My new, personal style fit in perfectly: short, funky hair and lots of trendy garb. Technically, Chaos was a lounge because they didn't have a cabaret license, but that was what made it great. They'd wave us past the velvet ropes. I don't know why, but I just hit it off with the right people and always ended up knowing someone there. We'd show up, and the manager, Theo, would be wearing a cowboy hat and surgery scrubs. He'd take us straight in, up the winding staircase to the VIP section.

Inside, the music was pulsating all the latest European house and techno. Celebrities up the wazoo. You weren't allowed to dance at Chaos because of the cabaret license, but they'd let the regulars get away with it, up on one of those velvet cubes, just gyrating away. And there were so many beautiful women: models, actresses, daughters of models and actresses. It was just mind-blowing.

At this point, I hadn't had a steady girlfriend for nearly three years. For me, this was my opportunity to *live*, my belated coming-of-age. So, suffice it to say, I made up for lost time. But I was a far-from-perfect Don Juan. In 1997, I was still living in my tiny closet apartment on Sullivan Street. Whenever I brought a girl home, it was hilarious because the size of my bedroom made us feel like hamsters in a shoebox. The walls were so thin that the neighbors could hear everything that went on.

The party at Chaos eventually moved to Spy. From there, I discovered Float. Float was the place that ended up becoming the site of the infamous club scene in the CNN documentary. Through it all, there were many late nights. I'd work until midnight or 1:00 A.M., go home, take a shower, head straight back out, meet up with friends, and then head out to the clubs. I'd go out four times a week, usually Wednesday, Thursday, Friday, and Saturday. At 2:30 to 3:00 A.M., I'd leave the first club and go to another one called Twilo. The music was amazing. Everybody was half-naked. Neon lights were flying. I'd never seen this before, and it was phenomenal.

During the summer of 1998 before the IPO, life for me turned into club land. The nights were unparalleled, and everything was about the music: house, trance, ambient. Even Egan got into it. He'd already switched over to an all-black, neo-chic wardrobe and bought himself a plush, multimillion dollar apartment in the Trump Tower. But when he started asking me what Oakenfold trance CDs he should buy, I nearly fell over. I don't know if he genuinely liked it or if he just thought it would help him change his image. Either way, when I was in close quarters with Mike and the bankers, I'd put on my earphones, shut my eyes, and relive those crazy moments in the clubs.

I'd never really clicked with the whole fraternity, beer drinking, thing in college. I was studying physics and computer science. For God's sake, I was starting a company in college. But in Manhattan, it just changed, and the tables completely turned.

Then there was the after-hours scene. Sometimes, around 4:00 in the morning, we'd go to Coffee Shop in Union Square for a burger. Or we'd go to Blue Ribbon for rich foie gras on sweet, perfectly toasted brioche. Around 5:00 or 6:00 in the morning, we'd head to someone else's place, close all the curtains, sit around the table, and watch old reruns of *James Bond*. Our enemy would be the daylight. That was the one thing that killed the vibe.

> > >

The bizarre thing is that I never spoke about theglobe.com to anyone. I just didn't talk about it. It wasn't my style. I'd rather ask people what they were doing. I was so much more into discovering New York, meeting people, and finding out what other folks were doing. That little geek feeling always seemed to surface when I brought up what I did. Most of my friends had no clue what I was really working on. It was a secret. A few people knew, but it was certainly nothing to show off about. Everyone else had normal jobs. People would always say, "The Internet? So you work with computers?" That was the extent of it. There was nothing cool about the Net at this point.

> > >

It quickly became obvious that between the endless work and non-stop partying, sleep would have to be eliminated completely. I'd come in every morning with huge rings under my eyes. But somehow, I managed. When you're putting this level of energy into your work and getting so much in return, you think you're invincible.

I'm not even sure why we worked so hard. As I said, the concept of being an Internet zillionaire was still so remote, so that certainly wasn't the goal. My principal experience as a businessman was the constant sense of being on the verge of death: always pushing as hard as possible and in constant denial of the inevitable.

Of course, after our IPO in 1998, life completely changed. But before the IPO, the idea of future wealth was just a vague notion. I knew about Netscape's Jim Clark and his fortune. But to me, that was still just some VC in San Francisco with 30 years of experience who hit the lucky number. I was just a nobody working on something that I loved. It was nice to have, but in my heart of hearts, I never really thought we were about to get rich.

What did I know?

7
THE ROAD SHOW
60 meetings, 20 cities, 10 days

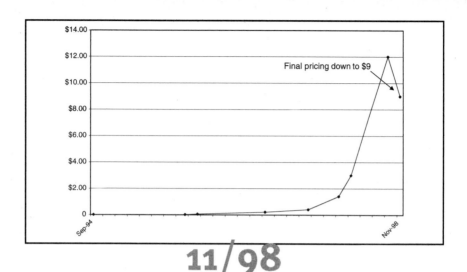

11/98

STOCK PRICE
(private company)

Chart labels: $14.00, $12.00, $10.00, $8.00, $6.00, $4.00, $2.00, 0 — Final pricing down to $9 — Sep-94 — Nov-98

T hey call it a road show. Think of it as two straight weeks of whoring yourself to every single major institutional investor you can, doing whatever you have to do to raise the money to go public.

Again, our timing was regrettable.

At the end of August 1998, just as we were waiting for the paperwork from the SEC that would approve our offering, the market began to collapse. There were 174 companies that had planned to go public but canceled their IPOs. People were canceling in record numbers—even Fox canceled.

Naturally, we freaked out. If we weren't going to go public, we'd run out of money. It would mean the instant death of the company. But the market kept dropping; even the word *recession* started being uttered.

Nevertheless, the SEC finally gave us the green light, and we filed our official documents in September. Still, we weren't exactly brimming with confidence. The question was should we even do this? Our bankers were telling us that everything seemed really bad. Bear Stearns felt the market looked like a disaster.

Todd and I decided to wing it because we really had no choice. If we put the thing off, we'd run out of money, and we'd already filed the documents. If we suddenly announced that we weren't going public, there'd be a negative wave of press. In our usual sort of brash way, we told them, "Oh, we can do it, we can punch through this storm." And so it was that we prepared to launch the road show in October.

The first thing we did was start practicing for our presentations. When I say that, I mean really practicing. We worked full-time with the bankers developing a full slide show—revenues, projections, competitive analysis, the whole nine yards. We also hired a professional coach for our presentation skills, this guy who came in and helped us with matters of diction and posture. We learned a massive amount. Todd, for instance, used to always stand stalk still and give his presentations like a robot.

My problem? The old genital clutch, in which your hands are clasped together, hanging right in front of your balls. "What are you trying to tell people?" the coach would yell at me. I moved my hands. We practiced for a month with this coach, going down to Bear Stearns, using their conference center. Before we went on the road, we did a mock presentation to the entire Bear Stearns sales force. They loved it and thought it was fantastic. We could certainly talk the talk: We could show a track history of how our quarters had grown and rocketed, the money we'd raised, the advertisers we had, the management team we had built. We could make everything look compelling.

Too bad it was just practice. The day we got on the road for real, the market dropped another 200 points. But we pressed on, hitting Connecticut, Boston, San Francisco, L.A., and a boatload of other places that I barely knew existed like Minnesota, Milwaukee—all these places where old, respectable institutions still thrive.

At least we traveled in style. Typically, we'd just get into Mike's private jet, which was one of the coolest things about this entire experience. We'd used his jet before to fly back and forth to Florida. The first time we got in, the hairs were tingling on the back of our necks—it was that phenomenal. Mike leased his plane from Wayne Huizenga, so this particular jet was a Gulf Stream III—nice and spacious with food service (Wayne also had several Lear jets, several Gulf Stream jets, several private helicopters . . . luxury-style helicopters right out of *AirWolf*).

> > >

Back in the day when it was just Todd and me running the business and we were running around trying to raise seed money, we always traveled ultralow budget. To save money, we would share a room and pray for good late-night movies like *The Fifth Element*, which made things a lot more fun. From our separate double beds, we'd talk until 3:00 in the morning. It was like being in camp or something.

But when we told our bankers to just put Todd and me in the same room, they looked at us sidelong—and we slowly realized that this might not look too . . . kosher. So we stayed in separate rooms. We had to get up at 5:00 or 6:00 A.M., go to breakfast (or to a breakfast meeting), and then attend six or seven more meetings a day.

We started in the Connecticut area with these Putnam Trust–type institutions and then headed over to Boston. On a road show, you start off small. The investors you really want are the big ones, and you need the practice.

The plan was to cover 20 to 30 cities in about two weeks. Those are business days, so that really means packing two and a half weeks into 10 or 11 business days. It's concert-tour, rock star dizzying. You start off in one city in the morning, do a few presentations, fly to the next town at noon, do a few presentations there, and either you stop there if you have more meetings the next day, or you get back on the plane, fly to another place, arrive at midnight or 1:00 in the morning, go to sleep, and wake up in another new city. You do a few more meetings, you get back on the plane, you head back out. You don't know where you are anymore. Very quickly, you no longer have patience to listen to new ideas being presented having to do with your business like, "Why don't we do this with our community?"

In fact, you don't have patience for feedback, period. Matter of fact, you don't have patience for anything. The only way to survive this is by isolating yourself, finding moments of perfect clarity and tranquility, isolating yourself mentally. As if.

Each one of these meetings could be anywhere from an hour to two hours, depending on their interest level. And then we'd zip around in limos because Mike brought his entire entourage (he'd quickly realize it was wasteful to have everybody there). It was nuts. Institutions normally meet with just the CEO and the CFO. With us, they got two CEOs, the chairman, three bankers, Ed, and others.

> > >

Our entourage may have been large and bloated, but our documents were certainly sleek. We insisted that our S1 be matte black with hip green graphics, which was very much considered taboo. But we wanted our form to stick out and attract eyeballs and questions, "What the hell is this?" Internet hype was gearing up, and we wanted to show that we were on that edge. A stale black-and-white document would have been just that, stale.

Despite all of this, Mike felt it necessary to always tell us how we could improve our presentation skills—every day, between every meeting. It was frustrating. Mike felt we needed the coaching but at the same time his part of the presentation was much less rehearsed. Every so often, we'd be in a meeting where they wouldn't quite get it or they had a specific question like, "Well, tell us exactly how this functionality would work." Mike would interrupt and say, "Let me take this one." There'd be a long pause, and then he'd start off with something like, "Imagine community like a banana split. . . ."

> > >

It was comedic, but it left us looking at each other like, "Who needs the coaching?" At this point, I should mention that we'd been diluted to owning 5 percent of the company. Mike owned 51 percent. Todd and I ran all the operations, but when it came to issues concerning equity, strategy, the big moves, final decisions on directions to take, we had to work with Mike. In a situation like that, eventually you start to relinquish real control. Right or wrong, we slowly began ceding our territory. Maybe the company would have done better if Todd and I had kept that control and always taken full responsibility for our successes and failures. Maybe we could have forced ourselves to develop these skills instead of sort of moving back a couple of steps and saying, "Well, maybe Michael will make things happen."

So we were out there on the road trying to drum up money, and the market just kept falling. Interest was progressively dropping from meeting to meeting. Their response was less, "Great management team, great presentation," than, "What the hell are you guys doing out here now?" The feedback wasn't very promising, but we just pressed on, even though no one was signing up for this baby yet.

And things got worse. At one point, we were in Texas and had to get to Colorado at some outlandish hour to meet the people from the Janus Fund or one of those institutions. We sat down with two uptight analysts from this institution who immediately started grilling us. Then sort of halfway through the meeting, another guy walks in, and he seemed to be even more important. So we started repeating everything again. And then, long before the meeting was over, one of the other guys left. Even more distracting were their pagers, which went off every few seconds. It was pure chaos.

I could see that one of the guys was clearly reading from his pager and totally ignoring everything we were saying. Finally, I asked what was so interesting. And the guy just said, "Oh, it's the market. We're down another 200 points." You could literally see a bead of sweat coming down his forehead. You could also see he was thinking, *Why the hell are you guys on this road show? Haven't you noticed 174 companies canceled their IPOs? You guys are a small Internet company, you're not some major telecom company. What the hell are you thinking?* Then they cut the meeting short.

Another time we flew out to L.A. to meet with some generic capital group. These guys looked like they'd rather be on the beach than meeting with us, literally. One guy was sitting on the other side of the table, staring out at the ocean. "Listen," he told us, "can you speed it up a little? I don't have much time here."

And they had asked to meet with us! Then they flipped to the back page of our book and said, "All right, thank you very much." This guy also dropped comments like, "Oh, yeah, my son's done some little rinky-dink project like this, too." Even Mike looked over at us at the end of that meeting and said, "Wow, what an ass."

Someone from T. Rowe Price once interrupted us to say, "I just want to let you guys know I think community is a really lousy business model. I really don't believe in it. I don't believe in Lycos, I don't believe in Tripod, I don't believe in GeoCities." And all this was said with a huge smile.

Todd and I were getting more and more frustrated. A road trip is something you only want to do once in your lifetime. It's that bad. But we were doing it, and right off the bat, we realized that we may have to do it all over again. And if we did it again, we'd be on the road with the 174 companies that had all canceled; we'd be part of a huge pack. That is if we were even *around* to get that chance.

It was looking like we weren't going to get the deal done. We'd originally been going out on a price range of $11 to $13 a share.

When you file to go public, there's always a range. If it's a good market and everyone wants in, you get the top of the range. If you're really good, they up the range. Not only does the price go up, but you can actually decide to sell more shares. In our case, we were already selling very little in the way of shares—3 million total—but we couldn't do it at $13, couldn't do it at $12, couldn't even do it at $11. We tried going all the way down to $8 without any luck. At least we learned one valuable lesson: When the market's dead, there ain't nothin' you can do about it.

Finally, after two and a half weeks with the market precipitously falling, we returned to New York. Todd and I were just so pissed that we'd gone through this whole circus. I don't recall exactly how much money we had left in the company, but out of the original $20 million, $8 million had gone to marketing and a good chunk of the rest had gone into beefing up the infrastructure to handle the 6 million users that were now coming to theglobe.com.

At best, we probably had enough money to last three or four months if we lowered the burn rate. But that meant all the momentum we'd built up would dissipate. And then there was the GeoCities problem. They'd gone all the way up to a billion-dollar company, but several months after going public, their stock price had dropped to well below their IPO offering. Now people were comparing us to GeoCities. They'd say, "How do we know if we buy you guys, you won't end up below your IPO price, too?" Meanwhile, Yahoo, Lycos, Excite, all of them had fallen to ungodly low numbers. It was bad, and the consensus was that we couldn't make the IPO. No matter how much power Todd and I thought we had, we couldn't do it.

I wasn't about to commit suicide, but on a scale of 1 to 10, 10 being joyful optimism, I was a 2. We'd gone through this four-year sprint, those pioneering days of the Internet. And now it would all be for nothing. We were going to vanish in one big poof of smoke. We would have to fire people. Todd and I realized that we were actually going to have to let go of a bunch of people. After so much ramping up, we were terribly bitter. Unfortunately, you don't get a grade for effort. When you're unlucky, you're just unlucky, and that was just the worst bit of luck we could have ever had.

The plan was to refocus on the business and figure out a way to get our burn rate way back down again so that whatever money we did have left—$5 million in cash—would last us a year. But even that would require so much cutting. No wonder I needed to go out at night.

By the time we reached mid-October, the IPO was officially off, and we convened in Mike's apartment in the Trump Tower. I remember standing in his phenomenal apartment with this spectacular view of the city.

Sharing this view with Todd, Mike, Ed, and me is Wayne Huizenga (from Blockbuster and AutoNation), Ace Greenberg (chairman of Bear Stearns), Bob Halperin (of Raychem and an early Intel investor), David Horowitz (of MTV and Warner Communications), and Ric Ducques (CEO of First Data Corp., also our latest addition to the board), all standing in a semicircle. In that moment, part of me was thinking, *Never mind all that's gone down. How did I ever get to this point where I'm standing here, a kid surrounded by these legendary, self-made billionaires? I wish I had a camera.*

Anyway, they all talked about what our options were. But the point was moot—we were really going to have to pull the S1 and cancel the IPO. But Michael, being as stubborn as always, wouldn't give in. "No," he said, "let's just leave the document out there. Let's just. . . ." He kept pleading and pleading, and kudos to Mike because it was his sheer stubbornness that kept the document alive, kept the door open for us to go public.

And what ended up happening? Bear Stearns finally said, "You know what? We'll take you guys. We'll buy all your stock for $6 a share." So we would be, what? A $50 million company. That would

Our first employees . . . pizza anyone?

Our first office, with plenty of leg room.

Todd and I take a well-deserved whiskey
break (1996).

Our death trap server room in NYC.

Traveling in style! From left to right: Frank Joyce (CFO), me, Mike Egan, and Todd during the IPO road show. Fall 1998.

Morning of the IPO . . . Ace Greenberg does his trademark card tricks in a futile attempt to relax us.

"$97!?" The pit at Bear Stearns where it all happens.

Todd, me, Mike, Ace, and Ed Cespedes.

Industry Standard/cover . . . three months of interviews for a teen heartthrob story.

At the NASDAQ headquarters, Friday the 13th of November 1998.

With Anders (my stepfather) and Mom . . . the night of the IPO.

With the love of my life, Jennifer (and proud wearer of our logo).

Our legendary press team (from left): Rebecca Seflow, Esther Loewy, Andrea Smith, Jen Zweibel.

By Lake Cuomo near Milan, during our secondary offering in Europe. May 1999.

Summer vacation in the south of France, August 1999, shortly before my Dad's illness was discovered. From left: Dad, Jen, Sophie, me, Monica, and Eric.

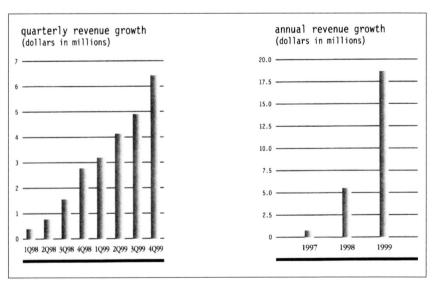

Our revenue performance as a public company . . . we were proud to step down on the heels of our best quarter ever.

make us a drop in the bucket. Even Mike was turned off by the idea, "No, let's not sell our entire company for 6 bucks a share. That's a steal."

So we passed.

> > >

Status report on theglobe.com at this time, late October 1998: Basically, we had been growing like crazy. Employee morale was phenomenal, and everyone was so excited and believed in our mission as if it was a religious crusade. Traffic was up; sales kept ballooning. Our sales were actually doubling from quarter to quarter—we had awesome growth. We were well on track to doing $5 million-plus in revenues that year, up from $750,000 in 1997. By the spring of 1998, we had fully embraced home-page building and our user count had ballooned. It was a wildly popular service. But we were still in our crappy little offices with our disastrous little server room, running in a little environment that was just a hellhole, and electrical wiring was sprouting everywhere like a crazy weed. We had people staffed 24/7 just to restart the servers at any moment because the site was crashing all the time.

> > >

Through all the head-spinning pre-IPO chaos, I was still going out regularly. On November 7, after another long night at work, I went with Julien, a buddy of mine, to a party that this 7-foot-tall Swedish girl had invited me to. I hadn't really wanted to go, but in the city, you never know what you might find or who you might meet.

The party wasn't particularly eventful. People danced, and I watched Julien try to pick up some other Swedish Amazonian, his head barely reaching her breasts as she listened to him from her regal height. At one point, I looked over and saw this beautiful girl. She seemed so elegant, with a beautiful, disarming smile. And I just did a double take, which is something you learn not to do in New York since just about every other person who walks past you on the sidewalk is worth a double take. I'd been single for four years: no love, no serious relationship, and given the way my business life was going, I needed something positive to happen in my social life.

That was Jennifer. A girl who grew up on a farm in Kentucky; she was beautiful and warm and intelligent. Even though Jennifer was a model, she was down-to-earth. We had this long, involved conversation that simply erased what I had been going through at work; I was putty in her hands. Then, in that classic New York way, the party sort of fell apart before I had a chance to get her number.

I thought I'd never be able to contact her, but by sheer luck, I ended up at Spy and there's Jenn with this large group.

This time I went right up to her and asked for her number, and luckily, she gave it to me. I pulled out my cell phone and popped those digits right in, saved. I went to bed that night the happiest guy in the world; a relationship seemed imminent. But little did I know Jenn would share with me two of the craziest years that anyone could ever expect to live through.

It must have been my lucky week. The following Monday, the market turned up a little bit, just enough that a few offerings that were in limbo suddenly went public. First Fox went public with a modest 15 percent run-up. Next, EarthWeb, an IT outfit I'd never heard of that was trying to compete with CNET, went public and blew up 250 percent. A couple other companies were lining up to go. There was a murmur bubbling through the market.

On Wednesday, November 11, 1998, I'm sitting behind my cheap little Cornell, '70s style, metallic desk, when The Call comes in. When I started to comprehend what I was hearing, I put the phone on conference, and Todd came over.

Our bankers were on the line with some unbelievable news. "Guys," they said, "you're never going to believe this. Everyone wants in the deal." I remember Todd and me looking at each other as though we didn't want to believe this. The emotional roller coaster we'd just been through left us loopy. If it hadn't been for Mike's eternal optimism, we would have pulled all our paperwork. Since it was still in place, there was a small chance we could get everything going for a quick filing.

Bear Stearns was less concerned about our emotional state. Every half hour, they kept calling us, "Guys, the demand is going up, going up. We've got to get everything worked out." We called everyone that had originally been part of the deal. Friends, family, everyone that I'd already told it was over, finished. I had to locate people all over the planet; people were on vacation, people were missing. We had 24 hours to get everything back together and refile all the necessary paperwork.

We didn't sleep Wednesday night. By Thursday, we were still cranking through the paperwork. On Thursday afternoon, bankers called to give us an update. "Guys," they said, "there's something like a 45 million share demand for your 3 million share offering." We were incredulous. The next question became—What do we do about the price? Since this was still officially at 8 bucks a share, we'd be raising half of what we originally needed. We'd only get $24 million instead of $40.

We called up Bear Stearns, but they refused to push it up.

"Why?" we demanded. "Goddamn it, look at this demand."

"We can't do it," they said. They'd already told everybody it was $8, and they believed that was why there was so much interest.

> > >

Nevertheless, that Thursday we really pushed and pushed (especially Mike), and finally, they came back to us and said, "Fine, we've got it up to $9 a share."

That meant we'd only raise another $3 million—this on top of our diminishing $24 million. Still, it was much, much better than nothing. And we really had no choice. On Monday, our S1 document would officially go stale and there was no more time. We could have sat there and insisted they let us keep pushing and pushing and pushing the price to $11 or $13, but the risk was too great. If the document went stale, we'd have to refile, and that's a minimum 30-day period, 30 days in which the market could tank all over again. Todd and I were just the ultimate pessimists and skeptics about everything by then. We had realized the window of opportunity was so small. It reminded me of when the Enterprise had only one chance to get through a wormhole and travel back 70,000 light-years. If we missed, the game was over.

So Todd and I shook hands and said, "$9 it is," and Mike agreed. We locked down that night and reprised the deal. By Thursday night, everything was filed and ready to fly.

Time for the Theraflu.

You may recall from the prologue what happened next.

At midnight, the clock chimed Friday the 13th.

PART

2

A PUBLIC FIGURE

life during internet mania and
a heavy dose of hackers!

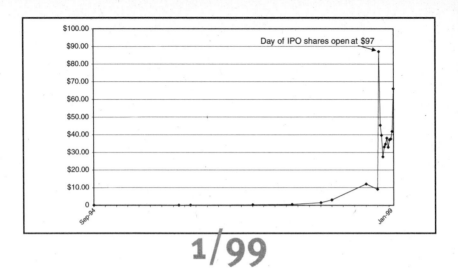

1/99

STOCK PRICE
(private company)

The night of the IPO, I kissed Jenn for the first time.

We went out to celebrate at Spy with Julien and Ahmad (my two best friends in NYC), and then about 20 of us came back to my house to keep things going after-hours. Jenn was sitting in a chair in my living room, and we spoke quietly for a while. She was still just a friend of a friend, and didn't have any sense of the enormity of what had happened to me that morning. As she got up to leave, we kissed, and it was the longest, most passionate kiss I'd had in years.

I went to bed alone that night, my head happily spinning. I remember how excited I was: I'd just kissed the woman of my dreams, and the whole IPO situation was, well, surreal. In a day, I'd been handed an entirely new life.

The next morning, I woke up with what should have been a major hangover but instead felt like this general sense of clarity. My first thought was, *Oh my God, it's done.* The press had already kicked in. The big feature in the *New York Post* was, "Geeks Make $97 Million." That day, Todd and I began to learn that people react to success in two different ways.

People were either genuinely excited by us, wanting to mirror what we'd done and learn from it. Or people were just instantly bitter, wanting everything in the world to ensure that we'd fail, which would make *them* feel much better.

More people than I imagined had heard the news. For instance, I remember leaving my building and catching my doorman smiling at me—everyone knew something big had happened to me in the stock market. Meanwhile, we were already preparing ourselves for the inevitable; our windfall was fine, but the reality was the stock could just as easily come down.

That Saturday morning, I began my life as a public figure in earnest, running a public company with a trading stock; nothing would ever be the same again. Starting that Monday, we were on everyone's radar, and all of our competitors would be gunning for us.

> > >

But enough of that—I know what you're thinking. What about the money? How does it feel to be worth $97 million?

Well, hold on. Let's look at the situation realistically. From a personal point of view, I'd have to be an idiot not to realize the potential for massive fluctuation. Despite our admittedly incredible price, we obviously knew that things were a little unstable at best. After all, we were supposed to go public at $9, and then we hit $87 and went up to $97. That Friday alone, our stock had fluctuated between $97 and $63, from second to second. And something like 16 million shares had been traded on a 3-million-share offering. Day One alone, our stock changed hands at least fivefold.

As much as I wanted this massive feeling of security and wealth, I knew that it wasn't going to last. If my own net worth could fluctuate up and down by $30 million from one second to another, I knew that over the course of two days, a week, a month, a market shake-up, that it could just as easily start rocketing down.

Still, that Saturday morning, I've got a big smile on my face. A day before, I was competing with my Ivy League friends who took the safe route, making the usual 100 grand a year, then 200 grand a year, then $300,000. Now all of a sudden, I'm worth $97 million. It's all over the headlines, all over the world, running on CNN *globally,* every other minute.

But at the same time, I had this eerie feeling. Because I was raised properly, I was taught, Don't let money change you. (Because it can change someone—in the sense that people will come after you.) So I already had this scary *Twilight Zone* feeling that people were watching me, waiting to see me start spewing money like a walking ATM. The doorman I'd caught smiling conspiratorially at me . . . what was he thinking? Would he expect a bigger tip for Christmas? And if I gave him less than, say, 150 bucks, would he call me a cheapskate and give me extra bad service despite the bonus?

I was frantically thinking, *What do I do?* They don't train you for this kind of thing, especially at age 24. Suddenly, I was scared that people would really start to change, that their perceptions of what my daily life was like would be wildly inaccurate.

The fact was that given the way things had been going, I'd spent most of my time getting used to the feeling that my whole career would falter imminently. Having sudden financial security really helped. I knew it would fluctuate, but I thought, *You know what? Even if it fluctuates $50 million, I'll still have $47 million.* I felt like there was plenty of padding and comfort, and even though I wouldn't be able to sell for ages, I'd be fine for a long time.

What did I know?

I spent the weekend at lavish dinners because we all wanted to celebrate. Suddenly, all my old friends and the new ones I'd met had grown over the past 24 hours. We were in a state of total euphoria.

Meanwhile, my friends and family—the ones who had purchased stock—were flipping out. People who invested 10 grand, acquaintances that I'd coaxed into getting in, all of whom had been fairly reluctant, suddenly made $100,000 that day, two years' worth of salary right there. And so we went out again to Spy. Everyone's happy, they bring us our own table, there's champagne, the booze is flowing, and I'm so excited because all these friends have just made a ton of money that they never even slightly expected. Of course, I ended up with the tab even though I didn't have any more cash than before.

That's the other perception problem that comes with a very public offering. Everyone thought I suddenly had $97 million sitting in a briefcase under my bed. Not true. Not even slightly. The fact is there was *no* cash. There was no real money, thus I couldn't change my lifestyle even if I wanted to. But everyone wanted so badly to believe it was real. It was difficult, especially during that first weekend, not to believe it myself in some abstract way. So, I played the part, which meant spending a lot of money on dinner, picking up tabs for cocktails, champagne, and having dinners at a lot of expensive restaurants who wouldn't have hired Todd and me to wash their dishes just a few years before. At the same time, I suddenly had people looking at me and whispering about me. Often, there was someone at my ear who I didn't know very well telling me something I wasn't really paying attention to. Forget that it became old very quickly, forget that there was no real cash, it was impossible to deny the sudden and overwhelming sense of power that came with several cocktails and the thought that somewhere out there I had $97 million. Tom Wolff's "masters of the universe" phrase suddenly became a lot more relevant with that kind of paper wealth behind me.

> > >

By the Monday morning after the IPO, my euphoria had evaporated and turned into pure high anxiety. I knew that at 9:30 every morning, the TGLO ticker would start moving, and everything we did would be a matter of public record. I didn't know how to run a public company. Mike had never run a public company. It's amazing how a lot of these billionaires get rich by selling their private companies to other companies; most of them never even think about going public.

Think about it: For the 5,000 public companies on NASDAQ, there are 10 million that are private. Being public is actually a rare experience. And as much as people like to lecture, they don't really necessarily know. Thank God Wayne Huizenga had run a public company as had several other guys on the board. They could give us some real advice. But none of them had done it at age 24. And it didn't seem like any of them had spent much time thinking about what that might be like.

Perception is everything. That's the scary part. If people think you're a gray-haired guy with a nice stable family, a plush house in the Connecticut suburbs, and your daughters ride ponies on the weekend, they get this feeling, "Ah, yes, my money's with a solid experienced guy."

Conversely, you wouldn't give your money to Groucho Marx. You wouldn't trust him even if he was the most brilliant accountant in the world. This was the sort of feeling that Todd and I started having. People still were skeptical about our youth, even though we'd just made them a 1,000 percent return in one day.

That became the back story of our IPO: a wildly fluctuating stock and 20,000 shareholders wanting to know what we were going to do. "What are you going to *do? Why are you so young?* What the *#!@ have I done with my money?" The truth was that there was so much sudden responsibility on Todd, myself, and the whole management team that we were all a bit scared. Nevertheless, we all jumped right back into business and got ready for the long road ahead.

For Todd and me, it was a pleasure getting back into the meat of running a company. A day would start with Todd and me catching up on the market news: *Wall Street Journal, New York Times,* CNET, and a dozen other sources. We always felt the need to be scanning the industry, waiting for any new blips to appear on our radar, such as new competitors, new financing, new killer apps being developed, and so on. We'd often then go visit every one of our competitors' Web sites to see what new products or services they'd launched, how their services worked, and even to speak with their users to uncover what they liked in particular.

Todd and I shared many responsibilities, especially when it came to the major corporate decisions such as what products to develop, strategies to pursue, new management to recruit, new financing to complete, but we also had our own personal interests. Todd's was to manage the financials, something he'd done since the company's inception. Although he had gradually delegated this to our growing financial staff, Todd still liked to double-check the numbers, making projections of revenues and expenses. Although I liked examining financials, too, I had a greater preference for scanning site statistics: how many users visited, average time spent, most downloaded pages, conversion from visitors to registered users, effectiveness of advertising banners, and so on. I loved playing with stats and equations, which was probably a lingering trait from my engineering days. I'd create massive Excel charts and input pages and pages of data with the most minute details imaginable. I'd then play around with the charting functions and try to analyze the data from every conceivable angle. I did this so often that Excel charts were constantly floating around in my head.

We'd often have weekly and daily meetings with our senior managers to hear status reports on product enhancements, sales reports, and marketing plans. Todd and I loved getting into the details and being hands-on, probably to the frustration of many employees who would have preferred more autonomy. Dean was very useful at injecting himself in the middle and providing Todd and me with the info we needed whilst improving our communication capabilities with the various departments. Often, I'd walk around our office and do laps, stopping by everyone's office on the way, popping my head in to get an update. Sometimes, Todd and I would randomly bump into each other at someone's cube. I probably spent half my time sitting in the ad sales offices getting sales reports and then moving down the hall for a technical update with our tech guys.

Obviously, things were never the same as when we were a private company. Now, Todd and I had the extra responsibilities as CEOs of a public company. More time on the road, often with Frank Joyce (the CFO) and Dean Daniels (the COO), meeting with analysts, institutions, and the press.

That Thanksgiving, I took a long-deserved break and flew with Jenn to London. We'd been seeing each other for two weeks; she'd get to meet my mother and taste her turkey. We spent a few days in a hotel, and it was just wonderful. I felt like this was "it"—after four years of searching, I'd found my soul mate.

But business was still very much on my mind, which meant more stomachaches. My new allergies wouldn't be diagnosed for another two years, so I basically had no idea what was wrong with me. It was just so embarrassing. I was with Jenn, having these incredible beautiful moments, and every so often I would have to say, "Whoops . . . gotta hit the can."

> > >

After going public on Friday the 13th of November, our first quarterly report was looming. We knew this quarter was in the bag. We were growing like crazy, doubling the previous quarter's numbers. We felt really good about the numbers.

But there was another concern worrying us. Though our traffic had been ballooning, we never had the type of money necessary to really build the infrastructure at a decent speed. Now our site was perilously overloaded. Our servers were melting. We'd given some thought to finding a new high-tech facility to off-load everything and build from the ground up, and now we dove into this plan on the double.

Thanks to our chief tech guy, Vance Huntley, we found a facility in Staten Island called the Teleport. It's a state-of-the-art maximum-security facility way out in the boondocks with all these massive satellite dishes, a no-fly zone, and infrared barriers around it.

By the time we were prepared to break down our New York office and make the move, our server situation was critical. We were still running in this dangerously overloaded room; at any time the servers could literally melt, which would take us off-line. This scenario, which had happened before, was now a recurring nightmare. We announced to our frantic tech team, "We're a public company. We have 20,000 shareholders. At no point in time can our site just go off the air!"

In October, before the move could happen, we had our worst technical crisis to date—we lost our home page service. We had millions of people with home pages on our site and about 6 million at the time visiting the member pages. All of a sudden, the number of pages was plummeting. The traffic was overloaded. And we're yelling, "What the hell's going on?"

It took us about 72 hours to diagnose the problem. The symptoms looked like those of a Denial-of-Service, one of those monumental attacks that we've all heard about. The same kind of attack that took Yahoo down. That took CNN down. It took the CIA site down. It's an attack in which computers are commandeered from all over the world, broken into by hackers who install little sleeper programs that when activated act like a military assault. The hackers have a command-and-control center, and someone sends an order out around the world, turning these sleeping Unix servers into secret agents. They receive the attack command and hone in on a given location.

The computers create false requests at a million attacks per second. You take 1,000 computers, and now you're dealing with a billion attacks per second, then it climbs up to a trillion attacks per second. Each of these attacks are false requests coming from a false address. So it's not like you can lock out addresses because every one of them is false. These attacks come far faster than the servers can possibly handle. They can't handle the load, and they crash, hard.

Now this was happening to us. The good news was that investors and users could still come to the front door of theglobe.com and visit the main site. But if they tried to go to a member page or create a member page, they couldn't do it. And that's where the bulk of our traffic was concentrated at this time, which meant all our advertisers on those pages were going down, too. So not only is the traffic down, but users are getting pissed because they can't access their home pages and advertisers are getting really pissed because their ads aren't being shown. Bottom line: This was going to impact revenues.

And it was happening in real time. Our tech team was spazzing. They worked on weekends; vacation time was a joke. They were ready to implode, their multitasking capacity having reached critical mass. The quarter's about to close, and we were ahead of the thing, but now, every day we're down, revenues are shot. We were now going to miss our first quarter, and we were in absolute hysterics. It was a travesty in motion.

Vance, our first employee and now our chief technology officer, was ready to collapse. The workload was killing him. Then, after an entire month with no sleep, Vance vanished. He didn't leave us an e-mail. He wouldn't pick up his phone or his pager; he simply vanished. Dean was just marching around the office like a lunatic. He had only come on board two months before as COO, and he kept saying, "This is tragic." We just hoped that Vance was still alive.

Then another tech guy, a brilliant hacker who could diagnose any problem, vanished as well, after a sleepless week. They were dropping like flies, and we still couldn't fix the problem. Is there a place where these techies go after they snap?

And the problem was compounded by the fact that our setup was so bad. We had so many critical points of failure that one little attack on a single area would create a chain reaction, and the entire system would go down. It was impossible to find which machines were being attacked, let alone know how to fix it, or more important, identify who was doing it. And why.

Of course, we had to figure out who wanted to destroy us. We tried to eliminate all the variables. "All right, is there any way we can locate who the hacker is?" "No. There's no given address." "Okay. What are the motives for someone wanting to take us down? Could it be some random group out there who is jealous that we're worth billions of dollars?" "No. That's unlikely. There are companies out there that are far bigger." Yahoo and all those other outfits were way bigger than us.

We considered a few potentially disgruntled employees, but we knew it was a long shot that the attack was personal. The few people who had departed on bad terms had been able to flip their stock, and would you really bother to exact revenge on a company that's just handed you $1 to $3 million?

We called the FBI. We tried to see if they had a special division that could help us out with cybercrimes. They said they would look into it, but they needed more information. We were talking to the head of their cybercrime division, and he was just as frustrated. Meanwhile, we're sitting there and our business is decomposing page by page in real time. What do we do? The FBI guy finally said, "Fellas, I recommend you hire a private-detective firm."

We hired a firm called Kroll & Associates, and they proceeded to trail another former tech guy 24 hours a day. They trailed him through the evening, through the day, and took pictures. They would deliver fake packages to his new office to see who was inside, what type of receptionist worked in his office, stuff like that.

Meanwhile, I started doing my own online research. I found out who his internet service provider (ISP) was. Through his ISP, I found out what his location was and what type of bandwidth he had. Then I went through our log files, trying to pick out Internet Protocol (IP) addresses. The idea was to see if he had been visiting our site or if he'd left himself any back doors into our database system so he could change things around. All I could tell was that he'd been frequently back to our site.

Kroll & Associates ultimately found nothing. They'd followed him to parties, and they followed him to his house. But they couldn't get any concrete information to give the FBI. There was simply no proof of any wrongdoing. So we called it off, but for approximately three weeks our servers were constantly shutting down.

Then, like a cowboy riding out of the fog, Vance came back. He was sorry—he'd completely lost it. We looked at him, "What the hell?" But we couldn't yell at him. Who could really blame him? He had worked more tirelessly than anyone I had ever met. He was the only authentic technical genius we had and the only person capable of counterhacking the hackers, but like anybody else, he had his threshold.

Shortly after his return, as suddenly as they started, the attacks suddenly stopped. It may have been because we fixed a few key components in our network that managed to dramatically reduce the impact of the attack. But the trouble just seemed to stop, and the number of pages started going back up. Then, we moved our servers fast as hell to Staten Island.

The new setup was as cool as the old place was crap. We created the most phenomenal state-of-the-art facility. There were raised floor, automatic air-conditioning, fire suppression systems; the place looked like the CIA, right down to the rolling tapes and rows and rows of black cabinets. Every single wire was perfectly labeled. It was all symmetrical; everything was doubly redundant. If anything went down, we could flip over to the new systems in real time. We spent millions to make sure this baby would be boss.

In the end, we finished the quarter with a 10 percent drop in our total traffic. Still, we made our quarterly projections. That may not sound like much, and if you're a private company, who gives a hoot?

But when everyone's watching, and you miss by a penny, it can crush your stock. Ten percent? My God! That could be the difference between hitting your numbers and missing them by a mile. The first quarter is the one you obviously never miss. You just don't do that. It would destroy your whole business.

We made it, but it was close.

That was just November.

> > >

By Christmas 1998, we'd done tons of press and we were every-where—even Europe (a European press tour in the spring of 1998 had helped gild the lily). My family was so excited. My sister Maddy who'd been a starving artist her entire adult life had put $200 into the company. That $200 was now worth something like $20,000. My dad's net worth in the company was $10 to $20 million. No one had ever in their wildest dreams expected anything like this.

I was thrilled that all these people—friends and family—had made a bit of money. But they couldn't sell; that was the sad part. Bear Stearns had locked everyone up, even the small investors. Of course, the SEC doesn't require a mandatory lockup. This is some-thing that the banks ask for. The reason? They want to make sure that when institutional investors are brought in, no one in manage-ment just flips the stock and gets out, causing it to drop. Instead, they lock *you* up, get the institutions in, and then the institutions flip the stock.

> > >

And once our IPO was done, all of the Bear clients who were in on our deal were the same guys who would get to flip the stock the first day. It was almost a guaranteed money-making arrangement, regard-less of how much demand there was for our stock. As would most investment banks, they held the price, even though the stock could have shot up, and offered it to their preferred clients. (Ironically, many of the clients who profited most were the same ones who'd told us to get lost during the financing.) The whole IPO process is truly fascinating; but for us, in the thick of things, it was becoming disconcerting. Seals kissing sharks.

> > >

I knew the cash wasn't real, but I wanted to treat myself to something. I've traveled a lot, and one of my lifelong dreams was to fly first class. Since I was going home to Switzerland for the holidays, I inquired into a first-class ticket with SwissAir. SwissAir is a total monopoly—their prices are insane. It's $1,000 for a coach ticket. First class would cost me $7,000. "F*ck it," I said, "I'm doing it!" Never mind that I didn't have the actual cash. (I learned a valuable lesson: If you fly with a monopoly, you get the same pathetic service up front, too.)

That was my biggest perk, and my last one.

> > >

I spent most of late December in Verbier (in the Swiss Alps) with my family, even though I wanted to be with Jenn (she was with her family). In Switzerland, I was a hero. Any hometown is going to be proud of a favorite son, but I was Switzerland's first Internet millionaire. They treated me like royalty.

When I got back to New York, it was a different story. Jenn was staying in my apartment while in between apartments herself, and my love life was heaven. Elsewhere, the honeymoon was definitely over.

That January, Todd and I were still traveling like crazy. We had to keep meeting with institutions. They all needed to know right away—should they buy more stock? Should they sell their stock? We had to quickly digest the practice of public accounting and prepare for our next report. We'd never done any of this before. We studied quarterly conference calls by other companies. We listened to Yahoo over and over. How did they do it? Who speaks? Is it scripted or not? We had to understand everything.

Then there was the question of who gets to attend the conference call. One hundred institutions? Several thousand investors? We didn't know. And, of course, the stock had fallen. Like any stock that goes up 1,000 percent, we'd come back down. In those first few weeks, we'd fallen and fallen and fallen. By the end of January, we were somewhere around $22 a share, down from $97.

We knew the whole thing was inflated, but we couldn't help but take any downward momentum personally. We'd seriously think, *Oh, God, what are we doing wrong?* It's ironic because, as anyone who's been in this position knows, a stock can take on a life of its own, but you can't expect people to stop drawing conclusions. When we started going south for the first time, just a few weeks after the IPO, some friends of mine told me, "Oh, you guys have fallen to $22. I guess business isn't going well." We hadn't done squat! Nothing had changed. But that's a simple reality no one seemed to get.

Our stock fell, of course, because the people who had stock at $97 thought it was overvalued and sold it. They sold it for $87 because that's what someone was willing to pay for it. And then those who bought it at $87 sold it at $77, or someone who had bought it at $9 and made a killing wanted to sell it at $60, and somebody was will-ing to pay $60. At that level of volatility, your price constantly mixes and matches, and it keeps dropping, dropping, dropping, with no apparent correlation to the daily business. It was like bad voodoo.

As our learning curve evolved, our second philosophy was, "Don't check the stock every day." Fat chance. I'd secretly be checking our price every five minutes, refresh, refresh, refresh, refresh. Todd would say, "You watching the stock, Steph?" "No. Not me," I'd lie. And, of course, I could see Todd clicking away, refresh, refresh, refresh, refresh.

But as I said, it was all new, and despite the fear and the stom-achaches, it was exciting. At that point, even at $22 a share, it was hard not to be excited when we knew that, theoretically at least, we had a net worth still over $20 million. It wasn't $97 million, but you know what? It was still in the multimillions, and I was, what, 24 years old. I felt pretty damn secure.

> > >

And so it was, with this newfound security, that we began life post-IPO. We finally felt we could control the company's market cap. We had the money to properly build the business, show massive growth, and watch the revenues climb. The stock stood to be positively impacted. Suddenly, Todd and I were thrust into the limelight, poster boys for Internet success and Internet excess.

The reality was, for the first time ever, the stock market had become a giant game. Like some very serious, very compelling PlayStation game with these huge, real-world stakes. For the first time ever, IPOs alone were getting all this press, and everyday folks were suddenly rabidly interested in the market. In a sense, Todd and I might as well have just been innocent bystanders. The thing had its own life, and when it flagged, the press played it up more than ever. The term had not yet been coined, but we were watching the dawn of *Internet mania*.

In the spring of 1999, it exploded. What does this all mean? What *are* Internet stocks? How are these things valued in the first place? Everyone thought there was a whole new set of rules at work.

It's ironic—a lot of people still have problems with this. I remember listening to Z-100 on the radio, and the DJ was talking about the stock market and how something can be worth $50 at one moment, and the next moment it's worth $40, and he's lost $10. The DJ wanted to know where his $10 *went*. As more and more regular folks started trading stocks, everyone tried to wrestle with this notion.

With Internet mania came the birth of the day trader. All of a sudden, there were 7 to 10 million day traders, trading stock online. It no longer was a matter of what you knew or about savvy institutions trying to figure out which stocks to buy. Where once-exclusive research held by the wealthiest people helped keep the rich getting richer, it was now a free-for-all. With the Internet, the very nature of research changed. Now things were impacted by rumors, stray comments, inside information, and the almighty opinions of a few powerful analysts.

CNBC took off, turning market coverage into the equivalent of sports broadcasting. The finance industry took on the drama of a hot auction. Everyone was watching. There was easy money to be made. The contagious nature of the mania became ridiculous. And Todd and I—even Mike—started getting infected. Running the business was subconsciously becoming secondary. For a good three to six months, it felt like the only thing investors cared about was for us to get the stock up.

Suddenly, Todd, Mike, and I were like drill sergeants. "Let's push it up! Let's push it up! Let's push it up!" Then we had a great first quarterly result: We blew away earnings estimates by some 20 to 30 percent. The stock picked its way up. We went back from $22, up and up. Then GeoCities, the largest home-page–hosting site, was bought by Yahoo, and that alone thrust us way up. By May, we'd worked our way back to as high as $84 a share. I was worth over $80 million.

But Internet mania was on the loose, and $84 a share wasn't enough. Todd and I had promised ourselves that we were not going to rest until this thing got to $100 a share. And it looked possible; we were on our way.

These were heady times. Now *everyone* was aware of the Internet, everyone wanted to get into a dot com and get rich quick. Companies were going public left and right, and not only were they able to get their stock price at the top of the range, they were able to move their range up twice as much. Instead of selling 3 million shares, dot comers could sell 4 million, 5 million, 6 million shares.

The end result of all this insanity was that we didn't look so flush all of a sudden. We'd raised only $27 million with the IPO—the bare minimum. Considering the competition was now raising $80 million, $120 million, $200 million, we felt pathetic. The worst part was that many of these companies were calling themselves communities.

One company was called iTurf. They were going to be a teenage community. This had to be the most bullsh*t thing I'd ever seen in my life. They had no users, no advertising, no commerce, but they raised $100 million! We were 10 times their size, infinitely better known, a better business, and we'd raised a fraction of the money they did.

We'd raised a fraction of the money that *everyone* after us raised. And that marked the beginning of our problems. "Oh, Christ. We have to compete, and they're all going to outspend us in every way. We *have* to raise more money."

To help the situation, another idea came along.

Mike had become heavily caught up in Internet mania. While we were still at $65 a share, he came to us beaming. "Guys," he said, "why don't we do a stock split?" Todd and I weren't exactly thrilled. Yahoo had waited till they were at $250 before they'd split.

But Mike had a plan. "It's very simple, guys," he said. "The theory is that everyone feels richer when they have twice as many shares. And that drives the stock up further." Our initial reaction was, "Well, do we really want to do this? What if we fall again, and then after the split, we're trading at $20 and below? There'd be such a negative perception." Todd and I were hesitant. We ordered a lot of research to be done by Bear Stearns and our lawyers, and they determined that the NASDAQ average for splits was around $50 a share. We were at $65, so we thought, *Okay, it's justified.* We were well above the average.

So right after we finished the first quarter, on March 31 during an interview on CNBC, we announced that we were going to do a stock split followed by a secondary offering to build up our war chest.

We were still stuck in a standard six-month lockup, which was the reason we still didn't have the personal riches everyone assumed we did. That was supposed to last from the November 13 IPO through May 13. Then the lockup was supposed to expire. But when we decided to do the secondary offering, we had to be locked up again, for another three months. (It wasn't until September that any insider could sell. And of course, by then, our stock fell to about $13 a share.)

As Mike suspected, the split did drive up our stock, but these drives are illogical to say the least. Why? Because the day traders rush in, going, "*Whee!* Buy more stock!" But it's completely illogical. Just because you've split your stock, it doesn't mean that anything has changed in value—there's just twice as many shares at half the price!

Still, things looked good.

Then I looked online.

>   >   >

Internet mania had also given birth to the ascension of message board culture. If you wanted information on a company, you could get everything you ever needed (and lots of stuff you didn't need) simply by checking into the Yahoo message boards.

When I checked our message boards for the first time, I couldn't believe what I was reading about my company. It was a cesspool. "Buy! Sell! The company sucks!" The general tenor of the discourse was astounding.

It was about to get worse.

One afternoon, I got a call from Ed. He wanted to give me a heads up. It seemed he and Mike were talking about something that had appeared on a message board. He said, "There's some sort of salacious comment on the message board that you might want to take a look at." I said, "What?" "Yeah," he said, "it's about you and some call girls." I felt myself starting to get sick.

Ed continued. "You know, Steph, we're not here to judge or anything, but you have to realize that as a figure in a public company, you've gotta be very careful. . . ." "Yes, I'm well aware of that," I said. *But what the f*ck?*

I went to the message boards and found it right away. There was a message posted by (of course) an anonymous user. The message was, "Watch out for this company, especially the CEO Stephan Paternot. I hear from the doorman in his building that this Paternot is a real sleazebag. A total sleazebag. He has call girls over all the time." The next message posted my home address, in case anyone wanted to send me some hate mail.

I was furious. To be told about this by my own board . . . and for them to assume that it was true? I was so pissed. I was also humiliated (and paranoid—did my doorman have it out for me now that I was worth millions?).

Needless to say, there had never been any call girls, so I was trying to think what could possibly give anyone this idea. I thought back to all the partying I'd been doing the year before. I'd been going out a ton. I knew all these great party people and lots of beautiful women. I'd invited a lot of these girls over. I'd always had beautiful *friends* coming over. Not call girls. These were my friends.

Then I thought about Jenn. In the weeks after the IPO, I had her over a couple of times. Now she was the most beautiful woman, tall and blond. And here I am, this young guy with his own apartment, having parties all the time. Suddenly, I could see why people would want to start spreading rumors about me.

> > >

I had to explain lots of other things to people. I remember sitting down with Todd on Fox's *Good Day New York* to talk seriously about the company, and instead having to answer questions like, "So, how does it feel to be so rich? Can I pinch you?" I actually got pinched on the air.

How do you answer a question like that? "It's, um, *fine.*" Then we'd try to explain. "You know, it's all in *stock.* We don't really have the money."

They didn't want to hear that. "Have you bought yachts?" they'd say. "Have you bought cars?" It was almost like they just wanted us to say yes to satisfy viewers and let people live vicariously. They didn't want to hear that I didn't have any money.

Meanwhile, a similar problem was affecting me in my social life. Very quickly, I started to realize who was a good friend and who couldn't be trusted. People I'd just met would act like my new best friends. Very quickly, they'd somehow work into the conversation, "Oh, yes, I'm working on this new business, and I was wondering . . . I mean, no pressure and everything."

They may have interpreted it as rudeness on my part, but these overtures had to be cut off quickly. The reality is that you have to set rules right away, even though you may look at someone and think, *Wow, I was once that guy.* When the word gets out that you look at stuff, you start receiving a thousand business plans a year. And since we were thinking about expanding, we had to be on the lookout. Of course, if you don't know how to stop and filter and be systematic in your analysis, you're going to make bad investments. Everywhere I turned, people wanted a piece or had something to show me.

Anyway, we survived all that—the crazy questions, the character assassinations, the "friends" coming out of the woodwork with business plans—and we just knuckled down and focused on the process of becoming a big independent company. We started ramping up content, adding news, stock quotes, e-commerce, everything. Yahoo, Excite, Lycos, and GeoCities had been doing all this, and we felt like we were in a race to keep up with them.

The reality was we started taking on too much.

9
ACQUISITION MANIA

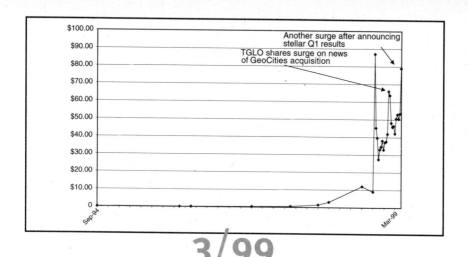

3/99

STOCK PRICE
(private company)

After the stock split, we turned our attention to chasing after the latest holy grail—e-commerce.

In the spring of 1999, Amazon had ballooned like crazy, and search engines, which had already been big, were getting way bigger. There was a six-month stretch in which companies just rocketed like I've never seen. E-commerce was the talk of the town. Analysts like Henry Blodget were hailing Amazon as a $400 stock. Everyone lusted after it, and acquisitions abounded. Which may explain why Mike uttered the following famous words, "We gotta buy a commerce company."

By the spring of 1999, theglobe.com had blossomed into a half-billion market cap. We'd entered that interesting phase in which you're able to use your market cap to swallow up other companies and still be open to considerations of being swallowed up yourself.

The logic was that if we wanted to stay big, we had to show

investors that we were moving along with the times. Forget that we'd just reached the big time ourselves. No matter we were in our diapers; now we had to learn to become astronauts. It was that fast.

Now, Todd and I *liked* the idea of acquiring companies. Mike began forwarding us info on a huge variety of companies, and what we quickly became concerned about was the particular companies we seemed to be chasing after. Todd and I would wonder why on earth he was forwarding these things to us. Granted, Mike never forced anything on us; he never told us we *had* to buy something. Which was really great, considering he was the chairman and majority owner. But sometimes he just forwarded too *many* ideas, whereas we just wanted to focus on a few and do those right.

One of the first companies Mike brought to our attention was called Buysafe.com. It was supposed to be a front door to all sorts of different shops owned by different companies. They were a mock little network where you could link from one site to another without so much as a common shopping cart. You'd end up going to all these different places; there was no brand identity. Moreover, what type of a name is Buysafe? Is that something people are going to get hot for?

Nevertheless, we looked at them. They thought they were worth $80 million. We took a close look, and this thing had what appeared to be growing revenues. They also had *very* low gross margins. They were practically giving away products because they were flush with VC cash. Something was very wrong. We backed away with our hands in the air. Good-bye, Buysafe and a good dozen other pretenders.

Eventually, we came across a company in Seattle that looked very clean and had a great brand identity. It was an online department store called Azazz.com. They had 14 different commerce categories. They sold everything from glow-in-the-dark doorbell ringers to Dirt Devil vacuum cleaners to Palm Pilots. We flew out, and Azazz proceeded to give us the best presentation ever. They were growing like crazy. They were going to do $7 million in revenues that year. With their growth and our traffic, we'd make beautiful music together.

One of the things Azazz most impressed us with was their self-proclaimed phenomenal personal shopping service. The idea was that you could click on a dialogue window and a personal assistant would pop right up to help you. It seemed nifty. Of course, it had absolutely no scalability capabilities. What if 1,000 users wanted to shop at the same time? You'd have to have 1,000 customer support people. Still, at the time, it all looked sexy. Mike liked it. Todd and I liked it. The entire board believed in it. We decided, "Let's do it." So, we negotiated a pretty hard deal. The initial price we'd worked out with them was $15 million in stock—that was 5 percent of our company.

Right as we were closing that transaction, over the wire there was a flash of breaking news. GeoCities had just been acquired for $3.5 billion in stock by Yahoo. Now, at the time, Yahoo was rocketing, so essentially that transaction became worth $4.5 billion overnight (and if you look at where the Yahoo stock price would eventually go, GeoCities essentially became worth something like $20 billion). There was something very wrong with these figures. Their revenues had been about $5 million a quarter. *Our* revenues were about $5 million a quarter, too, but *we* weren't valued at $4.5 billion.

And thus began the era when we started learning about the injustices of how valuations are determined. Everyone thinks this process is mathematical and empirical. The reality is that there's more fuzzy math to this whole thing than you could possibly imagine. There is no logic. Seriously. In many respects, your net worth is nothing but the reflection of the mood swing of some analyst's emotions.

When GeoCities was bought, everyone zoomed in: "Who's the next community that's going to be bought? theglobe.com! Buy! Buy! Buy!" Literally overnight, our stock started to rocket. We exploded all the way back up to $84 in the course of one day. Up from $30! A huge swing. The press was all over us, "Well, do you have any comments?" Publicly, we said, "Well, we think it's great." But the truth was one of our competitors had just been swallowed up and now enjoyed the backing muscle of a much bigger player.

On some level, we were pleased. The rationalization was, "There'll be no more focus on their brand. There will be no focus on GeoCities as an individual company. They'll lose market share."

But privately, I was scared sh*tless. First, it meant GeoCities would be there forever; it also meant that if we didn't capitalize on the whole acquisition fever fast, people would think theglobe.com was getting left behind. That could have a vast negative impact.

Still, our market cap rocketed. Suddenly, since we'd worked a fixed ratio to buy Azazz, that $15 million we were buying them for was now worth $45 million. This was totally unjustifiable. We were not going to buy them for $45 million in stock. They had no revenue because they'd virtually been created overnight. They had no market leadership and barely any audience. The pitch had been great, but, damn it, it was not worth $45 million. And this wasn't simple hubris. At the time, we had over 8 million users. We were one of the market leaders. We were producing at least $1 million a month in revenue.

So, we renegotiated. We were able to get the price back down to maybe $25 million in stock. We closed the transaction; everything seemed great. Of course, shortly thereafter, when we sent over our transition team to Seattle to meet with them, we started to realize that they were viewing us as big Wall Street corporate titans, like stiff, money-hungry, megalomaniac types. They seemed to have this vision of themselves as the cool little entrepreneurial wing of the company. I said, "Hold on. Have you seen our office?"

Now, when Yahoo took over a company, there was no question: That company was moved to California and rolled into their organization. Half the company was fired, and either you got on board or you got out. They had a real tough management style. Typically, Todd and I were more of the philosophy, What does it take to keep them happy? We said, "Hey, you know what? They're happy out there. Let's not bother them. Plus, it will keep our costs down by not having to relocate them." But it also meant we'd have to run two separate offices.

After we bought Azazz, we shuttled all our shoppers to them. We probably drove 250,000 users a month to these guys just like *that*, but sales weren't really picking up. So we started getting frustrated. "What's going on? What do we need to do? Is it time for a redesign?" They wanted to keep a separate look and feel, and we said, "No, let's create the same look and feel. There's no reason to make our users feel like they've gone to a completely different site. They're not going to necessarily trust a different site."

That meant butting heads more with Azazz. This got very frustrating very fast, and we spent an inordinate amount of time just trying to manage them. Once, we went out there with Mike and listened to one of their guys talk about his sales strategy, which went something like this: We buy a product for $100 and sell it for $80, thus losing $20. He smiled serenely and waited for our response.

I had to make sure I was hearing correctly. "Um, well how do you *make* money that way?" "Simple . . . we scale up." "You scale up?" With scale, they planned to win. I found myself thinking, *Cool. If you scale up a $20-per-product loss, you will end up with losses of $20 billion. That's just fantastic.*

It was a bad dream. This was not going to work, and we were stuck with it. Remember, when the e-commerce craze hit, every Internet company was selling products for less than cost. Literally, they were giving away product to beef up numbers that were as arbitrary as the valuations that went along with them. Like the rest, Azazz was quickly turning into the same disaster. The worst part was that whenever you make an acquisition, the press is all over it and the analysts want your new financial numbers. They want to see new projections showing how big you're going to get. So, we had to give them new projections, and we started padding things. If Azazz told us they could do $7 million in new revenues this year, we'd tell the analysts we'd do $3 million with Azazz to give ourselves some breathing room.

This was when things started getting ugly. By the third quarter of 1999, Azazz was supposed to be producing $1 million in quarterly revenues. Halfway through the quarter, they had maybe produced $50,000. We were in total hysterics. We were pushing *our* guys harder than we could possibly push them, but we still weren't getting there. Azazz also had millions of bugs in their software—the thing would never work properly. From their perspective, everything was great for them in Seattle on their own internal network. From anywhere else, it sucked.

Moreover, in Q3, we had a weak ad sales month for July. That set us off on a really bad pace. We'd produced great previous quarters, but our sales team had simply dropped the ball. Combined with the fact that Azzaz had *completely* missed their numbers, it turned into an ugly third quarter. Now, we'd still beaten our earnings numbers because we kept our costs down. We beat EPS, and that's the number the analysts cared about most. In truth, it wasn't that bad. By Q3 1999, we were doing about $5 million a quarter. When we went public, we had only been doing about $800,000 a quarter. In short order, we'd ramped up like absolute mad. We were on track for $20 million in annual revenues, up from $5 million the year before.

But some people see things differently.

Despite our massive ramp rate, despite having beaten our own projected numbers, Bear Stearns gave us a scathing review and downgraded us. They were the only one of our four covering analysts to downgrade us. They'd been our lead banker and the first to drop a bomb on us. (Of course, shortly after we went public—a record-setting IPO, out the gates crushing all their revenue estimates—Bear Stearns pushed us like crazy, telling all their institutions we were the greatest thing since sliced bread.) Now, instead of a buy rating, they came out and put us at neutral.

It was the most insulting, infuriating situation. A downgrade is the ultimate slap in the face. When it came down to it, it meant a no-confidence vote, and when your lead banker does something like that, it really doesn't matter what any other analysts say. The press starts picking up on it, and most likely, you're dead meat.

Meanwhile, there we were, drowning with Azazz. To help alleviate stress, I developed a technique of drawing things on our big white board (something that would be picked up on by other people as well, as you'll see later). One of the things I drew was this huge dam filled with water. The water represented our user base and the massive revenue potential; the dam was Azazz, the name of which had now been changed to Shop.theglobe.com. On the other side of the dam is this little picture of Azazz's president. He's got a mini tap switched on, with this little trickle coming in, and he's got a glass. He's singing, "Ooh-hoo, guys, things are going great. The glass is almost a quarter full, it's a great trickle."

For Q4, we needed Shop.theglobe.com to produce $2 million in revenues. So we came up with all sorts of coupon strategies, discounted products, anything to make that number. Remember, in 1999, revenue was still king and losses were still . . . acceptable. If you lost money but grew faster still, all was forgiven. Take About.com. They were one of those classic Net companies. Just after they'd gone public, they raised $80-plus million and spent $20 million in one quarter on advertising. They were losing a ridiculous amount of money, but the analysts just kept giving them top reviews.

So, based on that theory, we did an abrupt about-face and said fine. Instead of spending less and less, like we'd done during the ramp up, we'd launch a massive ad campaign. Thus, in late 1999 we announced our new $27 million ad campaign, all to show our aggressive new commitment to growth. Like lemmings—and during the Net bubble of the late 1990s it was difficult to truly differentiate lemmings from trendsetters, copycats from change agents—the analysts loved it. And as usual, our timing sucked. The mentality of the industry was changing so fast. By the time we started implementing the new campaign at the end of Q4, the Internet mania had reached its crescendo. By January 2000, people were officially sick of losses and things started really turning around.

We'd also poured a huge amount of money into Shop.theglobe. com. We shoveled so much in that by the end of the fourth quarter, we'd generated that precious $2 million in revenue. But at a cost of nearly $6 million. The losses were just *ridiculous*.

In January 2000, our CFO, Frank Joyce suggested we wind it down and take a write-off. At first, Todd and I were dead set against it. But the truth of the matter was that our stock price was shrinking so fast we could never move fast enough, we could never get ahead of that investor hype curve. We got rid of senior management and brought in a heavy hitter from Eddie Bauer. The impact was felt immediately and sales really picked up, but it was too late. Despite rocketing revenues, the margins were just too small and caused us to lose money at a faster pace. In the end, we made the tough decision to shut it down.

> > >

But Shop.theglobe.com was only one of several acquisitions. We made another major purchase in March. The Attitude Network, a gaming network comprised of Happy Puppy (a leading U.S. site), Games Domain (a leading game player in the United Kingdom), and Kids Domain (a leading kids site in the States). Attitude Network seemed like a reasonable acquisition. The business plan was there because they'd been around for several years growing their site. They had some revenues, and they were already talking to Lycos. Then Lycos walked away, and we pounced.

It was a no-brainer. They had an advertising-based model very similar to theglobe.com: users show up; they spend time; you sell targeted advertising in the games category. Moreover, we thought games were awesome. It is first-mover-type audience for hard-core

Internet users, and that was great for community. There's nothing like gamers sitting in chat rooms, talking up our other games and citing them in their own Web sites. They added a perfect audience . . . a perfect business . . . that we knew how to sell. "Let's do it."

So we negotiated a deal just as our stock moved to the point where we were a $600 million company. We ended up buying Attitude for $43 million in stock—just under 10 percent of our business. That was a great purchase. That became Games.theglobe.com. Unfortunately, it turned out to be one of the only positive acquisitions we made.

Games Domain on the other hand (a U.K. subdivision of the Attitude Network), turned out to be the sort of thing that made Azazz look like fun. It was run by a couple of blue-collar blokes from Birmingham who seemed to think that everything America produced was *shite* and that everything that came out of England was *fecking fantastic*. Granted, they ran a tight outfit with 25 employees, but the average person was probably making $15,000 a year. Todd and I really believed that in the Internet space *people* were the asset, so we tried to accommodate a situation that was quickly becoming unbearable, a clash of transatlantic Internet cultures. In hindsight, Todd and I should have moved them to the States right away and demanded total control like Yahoo would have done. But we didn't.

> > >

Then there were the acquisitions we didn't make. It just so happened that one of Todd's friends was the CEO of Sunglass Hut. Now, at the time, they were a private billion-dollar company. Mike got wind of the acquaintance and wanted to turn it into an acquisition. "You know what?" he said, "The great thing about Sunglass Hut is that they're the leader in their vertical. You automatically know that brand and what they represent. Let's do it."

If we did make a move like that, people would accuse us of a lack of focus. They would think we were completely nuts. Todd and I would become laughing stocks. Now as I said, Mike wouldn't *force* anything on us, but the thing about him is . . . he's relentless. He just kept talking and talking and talking until the point where we just had to give up. He didn't force us technically, but it was exhausting to keep resisting him.

At this point in 1999, Todd and I were still at our old office, the barracks. The place was just falling apart. Even the elevator with its slow-clinking chain gave way a few times as we fell several flights. Mike would always sweep in with his full entourage, close the door, and sit with us on our rotting futon. "How's it going, boys?" he'd say with this big smile, flashing his baby blues. He'd rock forward, start talking, and Todd and I would glance at each other knowing that it was time to clear our schedules. Those conversations could go on for five hours.

With Sunglass Hut, I'd try something like, "Well, the reason it can't work, Mike, is the following. . . ." But Mike would always respond earnestly with, "Well then, how about this?" Then Mike would call a few days later and say, "So, boys, you made any progress on that deal?"

We really couldn't blame Mike's gut feeling. Sunglass Hut was a great company. If we could own them the way GE owns hundreds of different companies, we could do really well. The reality, of course, was that we didn't have the power. Yes, we were a billion-dollar company on paper, but we were just doing $20 million in revenue. We simply weren't in a position to start buying up new industries. That argument finally convinced Mike to give up on Sunglass Hut, but there was an infinite supply of other companies for him to obsess over.

One afternoon in the fall, Mike called to say, "Guys, I've got conversations going with Vitamins.com. They have stores all over the country, they're setting up online, and they've got $20 million in revenue. What if we buy them? I've spoken with their guy, and he's really interested."

We stopped that adventure, but the process continued. It was always like this. Mike would read some article at 5:00 A.M. in the *Wall Street Journal.* By 7:00 A.M., phone calls were in, voice mails, faxes. "Guys, what do you think? Please look into this. Let's have a full report." *Ugh.* Todd and I would put our heads down. I have much less patience and tolerance than Todd. Sometimes, I'd just start screaming. And on some occasions, Todd and I would have major arguments as a result.

> > >

In all fairness, we'd been at this with Mike for a while. Back in 1997, before we went public, Mike had some connections in the adult publishing business, which didn't surprise us at all—it seemed Mike had connections in every industry. They produced some sort of porno magazine. In short order, Mike set up meetings. Actually, Todd and I didn't think this was a completely outlandish idea. We could charge subscription fees, for instance, but we knew it would be difficult to manage. How do you maintain a separate little subdivision of your company for the scanning of porn photos? My stance was that either you're a porn company or you're not.

We met this one guy who was draped in gold chains; you could almost make out the porn stars dancing naked in the next room. Part of me wanted to take a look. The other, rational, part thought, *Wait a second here. Do we really want to get into this industry?* In the end, we passed. Professionally speaking, it would have been a bad move even though the porn business was, and still is, the most profitable venture going online since it would have prevented us from going public. I also knew I would have had a hard time explaining it to my grandparents.

> > >

In the fall, as our stock kept dropping, Mike said, "What do you think about theglobe.com buying AutoNation?" Now AutoNation, which was run by Wayne Huizenga, was the big car company that had bought Alamo. At first, it had gone way up in stock price, but then everything collapsed, taking with it a lot of Mike's hard-earned fortune. The car business has low margins, they weren't driving new business, and their price had plummeted. They'd sort of settled into their role as a $4 billion slow-growth company.

Mike thought we could buy AutoNation for a good premium. We tried to dissuade him. "God, Mike," we'd say, "we're having enough trouble as it is. We need to get down to the nitty-gritty of running our business. We need to start really figuring out how to get theglobe.com working better and not letting ourselves get distracted by grandiose ideas."

But he pushed and pushed, and Todd and I eventually said, "Okay, let's look into it further." We had such little experience, and that makes anyone start second-guessing. We'd gotten to a point where we'd say, "If Mike's so into this thing, maybe it is worth checking out." Mike wanted us not only to check it out but to save it. "You guys are the Internet wizards," he said, "figure out AutoNation's strategy."

So we'd sit down and try to figure out what to do to bring Auto-Nation into the Web-driven future. We came up with a bunch of ideas, and then Mike called up Wayne Huizinga and said, "Todd and Steph, tell Wayne your Internet ideas." God, we felt so awkward. Wayne's this massive businessman. He doesn't need two kids with an online community telling him how to run a car company. But we tried. Then Wayne, of course, answered, "Well, guys, we already spent a good year with my people strategizing over these things, and we think that's a bad move for the following reasons. . . ."

Ouch.

But remember—there's a reason why a zillionaire like Wayne Huizenga would consider listening to someone like Todd and me. There was a moment in the late nineties when the collective financial world basically said, "Bet *everything* in the Net business. And get yourself some Net kid to run it." If you were in healthcare, finance, whatever, everyone said, "If you're an Internet kid, you know how things work."

Hell, it happened with my dad, a successful (albeit old paradigm) businessman in his own right. Very quickly, he was asking me questions like, "Steph, what do you think about WebMD?" I responded, "Dad, I don't know *anything* about the healthcare industry." "But they're an Internet company." "So what? Okay, fine. Make sure that the banners are black and green so that people click on them." I mean, why not? For some reason, it didn't matter that we didn't know anything about the vitamin business or e-commerce. Actually, we really didn't know much about *commerce*. But it just didn't matter.

Now I'm not trying to cast blame on other people. Todd and I were the CEOs, and if CEO is truly where the buck stops, then we better damn well manage that. To Mike's credit, he is a brilliant entrepreneur with a proven track record. He has built multiple billion-dollar companies, and he has great ideas. Aside from some of the last few examples of proposals he made, there were many that were brilliant. He was fully onboard with the four acquisitions we did make and had many more great ideas to share with us. The only thing I'm trying to underline was that whereas he could keep on providing suggestion after suggestion, Todd and I had to execute them, and the only way to do that was to just pick a few targets and stick with them, no matter how tempting other new prospects could be. It's really our fault for not putting a stake in the ground and saying, "No, this is how it's going to be. We're going to stick with what we know." Maybe some of it can be attributed to our age, but that's just an excuse. Sometimes we just didn't take enough control.

After backing away from AutoNation, we'd managed to convince Mike that we needed to buy companies that were similar to us. So, with that in mind, we looked at other home page–building companies. Eventually, after a few near disasters, we found a company in California called WebJump. They were a professional Web-hosting service, and they'd grown a ton. We scooped them up for about $17 million in stock. After having dealt with several acquisitions already, we were getting really good at this. We had an entire mergers and acquisitions team in place headed by Ed. They would do all the research on the market segment of our target, do due diligence, meet with their management, go through a matrix of checklists, and then propose this to the management team and the board. Upon making the deal, Dean would then lead what we called the transition team into the acquired company and start integrating the new assets. We would bring in our top managers to meet with their top managers and rapidly start mixing and matching our protocols so that we could get to work. Acquisitions were great. Although cultural differences could often make them difficult to integrate, the benefit was that we could move at light speed and grow the company more aggressively. Again, everything with WebJump was great . . . at first. We appeared to be getting a tremendous amount of reach, along with the assets that come with new servers and traffic, all of which we transferred to our system. Of course, in short order we realized that the management out there was complete schlock. The good news was that this time we had detected this during due diligence and Ed, Dean, Todd, and I had decided just to buy their assets and not give contracts to their management. It was brilliant. We got all their valuable assets without burdening ourselves with these sketchy people. Shortly thereafter, we found out that they filed for personal bankruptcy protection, and we also discovered that they were running another site called Web1000—a massive porn-hosting service. We had to laugh. People are always complaining about accidentally getting into porn sites while online; we had managed to accidentally do *business* with these guys.

So at this point, we were now juggling three outside companies. Instead of just being theglobe.com, we were four companies with challenges that needed our attention every day of the week, 24 hours a day. We were absolutely exhausted, and the burden continued to build. The situation was becoming untenable.

Still, through January and February 2000, we tried to hunt down acquisitions that would grow the company and goose the stock. Our price kept dropping, even as our competitors—companies that were way smaller than us—were going public for 10 times the price we were worth. EToys was a multibillion-dollar company!

Come spring, we decided to beef up our gaming network. We found a company called Strategy Plus, which was a games magazine that had a subdivision called Chips and Bits, an e-commerce outfit. They were producing $12 to $14 million in revenue, and they were just becoming profitable; it looked fantastic. We scooped them up for about $17 million in stock as well.

Strategy Plus was based in Vermont, a seven-hour drive from New York. The first time we drove up to meet with them, there was a hailstorm and we nearly ran over a moose that had run across the road.

As always, things were fine at first. But very shortly thereafter, we realized that the founders had staffed the place with family members, giving it a perverse Swiss Family Robinson kind of vibe. It turned out that many of the financials were misleading.

By this point, our management team knew how to deal with this and we felt confident we could eliminate the problems at the top with minimal collateral damage. The biggest surprise was the reaction. Sensing their own mistakes and having heard that we were about to eliminate them, they literally took their money and ran, hopping on a plane to Monte Carlo. We were dumbfounded… Monte Carlo? Overnight, we sent up a team to manage this thing, just as the guys at Games Domain were getting in another tizzy. Todd and I were always pleased when we would hear from some of our friends at Yahoo that life was the same over there. Difficult at best, chaotic at worst. You just had to deal with it. Amazingly, there was still a light at the end of the tunnel. The assets of all our companies were good. Despite all our troubles, we'd ended up with the no. 1 gaming network in the world. And it was *profitable.*

As a result, we decided to officially scrap the whole e-commerce thing. We had just eliminated Azazz and taken a massive write-off in the spring. At least we stemmed all those losses, which was the right move.

But even though we were the no. 1 gaming network with tons of traffic, the problem was that everything we did was buried beneath theglobe.com stock prices. No matter what we did, we couldn't seem to convince anyone in the media that we were anything but a sad stock story. People simply knew us as a stock—they barely even glanced at what theglobe.com was doing or how fast we were growing, let alone bothered to consider our games. It was so frustrating. Little did I know it was going to get worse.

Let me give some sense of how we looked at the time. We'd gone from 80 employees at the IPO to about 120. By the time we completed our last acquisition in the spring of 2000, which was Chips and Bits and Strategy Plus in Vermont, we were 260 people.

We made these acquisitions, we were becoming a solid company, and we'd gone from $5 million in revenues in 1998 to $18 million in revenues in 1999. We were projected to do nearly $30 million in revenue the next year.

We were 20 times bigger than at the IPO date. But instead of being 20 times bigger than our *value* at the IPO date, we valued at 1/100th what we were at the IPO date. It was totally unjustifiable. And there's nothing we could say or do. Todd and I made plenty of mistakes, but most of the variables that affect market cap and perception are beyond anyone's control. We began to get our first taste of the soon-to-be-familiar sensation that things were spinning very much out of control.

This was something that Todd and I could have never imagined. Just a few years earlier, we didn't know what going public meant. Now we had 260 people dependent on us for paychecks and thousands more affected by a stock price. Despite all our troubles, I still felt like I was on top of the world. When I walked down the hallways, I'd walk with pride. I felt good about what we'd achieved. I felt financially secure. I remember thinking that for all intents and purposes, I had cash, infinite cash.

10
THE DOUBLE-EDGED SWORD

the media attacks my black plastic pants and
my "disgusting and frivolous lifestyle"

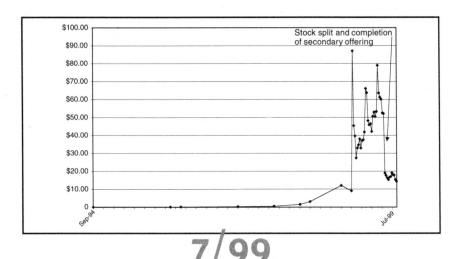

$100.00
$90.00
$80.00
$70.00
$60.00
$50.00
$40.00
$30.00
$20.00
$10.00
0

Stock split and completion
of secondary offering

Sep-94

Jul-99

7/99

STOCK PRICE
(private company)

Exactly why was the Internet such a hype machine? What allowed all these Web companies to raise huge amounts of money and attract all that rabid investment? I like to think of it as a kind of mass hypnosis: a massive, unshakable, institutional buildup of the notion that something phenomenal was happening.

Which brings us to the press.

> > >

From 1995 and thereafter, there was a very tangible sense in the business press that the world was changing. We were on the cusp of something revolutionary, something of a scale that hadn't been seen for millennia. As the Internet entered the public's vocabulary, so too did the notion that we were witnessing the greatest technological leap since moveable type.

It was a great time to be a reporter. So many crazy stories to write. Reporters on the Web-business beat seemed to have an insatiable appetite for those crazy Internet entrepreneurs and their amazing stories. Here were young Americans working so hard they didn't go home anymore. Here were people working around the clock feverishly, sleeping under their desks, bringing their pets to work, working in these completely postmodern conditions. This new breed didn't wear suits, and they didn't hold regular hours. People were turning their jobs into all-night cramming sessions for a crucial final exam.com.

We started reading about this, and it didn't stop. The public couldn't get enough. They had an insatiable appetite for this amazing new universe. They wanted to be in this astounding virgin world. Especially when they started reading about all the money being minted, the new fortunes made, and the head-spinning magic of inexplicable Internet stock valuations.

The reigning headline of the era was "Company with Massive Losses Is Worth $300 Million," and the reigning formula for determining the value of a company was multiple to its losses. The more you lose, the bigger you are.

Because this was the case, we became the quintessential Internet story, the global poster boys of Internet excess. Generally, the press reacted to theglobe.com—and by extension, to the whole Web—in two ways. The first was benign optimism: "How can this be? Two young kids running this huge company?" The other reaction was complete pessimism: "This shouldn't be. This is all *bull*, and it's going to burst. Just keep waiting, and the bubble will eventually pop." One hand wanted to build us up and tell our amazing story, the other hand wanted to tear us down. During the early days, we'd had some coverage, but the real explosion took place from the day of the IPO. From there, it progressed in surges and ended as a tidal wave that left us treading in its wake.

But long before we knew how to handle the press, we strolled blithely into their sights. My relationship with the media started out fairly pleasantly.

We did our first European press tour in the fall of 1997. We had scheduled interviews in the United Kingdom, France, Germany, and Sweden. The basic idea was to hit four countries in one week.

Though we'd go back to Europe in the spring of 1999, our first overseas romp was pre-IPO. We were hot at the time, and the Euro press had just been converted by the coattails of Internet fervor and its attendant IPO mania. We thought the timing was perfect as we'd be building our brand in Europe before the main Internet trend hit.

We began in England, where we quickly spent most of our time explaining how it was possible for young Americans to start these new businesses and why it worked more easily in America than it did in Europe. Naturally, people looked down their noses at us. I remember these staid British interviewers saying, "Righto. So, how do you *boys* do this?"

Still, we took on as many media outlets as we could stand. On any given day, we would do press from 4:00 A.M. all the way to about 6:00 or 7:00 P.M. We'd do two different BBC radio interviews, Sky News, BBC News on television, a few magazines, a few tabloids, whatever. Our public relations head, Esther Loewy, had packed in the meetings. There must have been 25 or 30 interviews in five business days. Since England is such a relatively small market, somebody would invariably recognize us from earlier in the day. And it actually affected traffic. We saw our U.K. audience grow from 200,000 users per month to 500,000 in the course of about a month.

After the United Kingdom, we hopped on a plane and headed to France. There, instead of stuffy Brit journalists, we found ourselves being interviewed in cafes through a haze of smoke. "Let's have some steak," the reporter would say. There'd be questions, but they were definitely more interested in eating and pointing out that the ketchup I was having with my fries was sacrilege. Meanwhile, the reporter got sauce all over his shirt, a cigarette dangling from his mouth, and we were sitting in the nonsmoking area. In France, the main question was, "Okay, so how much money did you make? $98 million right? That's nice, that's good." We left Paris, hopped on a Lufthansa flight, and headed off to Hamburg, Germany—a city without a center.

Surprisingly, the Germans seemed more relaxed, so we gave in and started drinking with the reporters, and the interviews became progressively sillier and sillier. Maybe that was why we got such good press. We did *Stern* magazine, *Der Spiegel*, and several other German publications, and they all had a wry sense of humor that really suited two Internet guys like us.

From Germany, we headed off to Sweden, and that was the most unique part of our Euro travels. I remember arriving in Stockholm at 2:00 A.M. We got off the plane, it was absolutely freezing, we drove along in a Volvo to the Grand Hotel, and there were icebergs outside. I remember thinking, *What the hell am I doing here?*

It turned out that the Swedes loved us. They'd already been writing all this positive stuff about theglobe.com, and they were just infatuated with us. Sweden was well known for being very wired, and somehow, we'd surfaced there.

Still, by the end of the tour, the back-to-back interviews had taken their toll. The endless repetition, repetition, repetition, started to become a blur. I couldn't even remember anymore what I'd said a half hour earlier, and the interviewers were starting to look at me funny. It couldn't have been that bad though, since our numbers went up in Sweden, too.

The press had been almost entirely positive. Seemingly victorious, we went home. One thing had become crystal clear to us: The more press we did, the more people heard about us, and the more our traffic grew. More traffic would lead to more advertisers, generating higher revenues. And, of course, higher revenues would make our shareholders happier. The best part about the press was that it was all for free.

> > >

After the IPO, the first thing Todd and I noticed was the power of CNN. Of all channels, of all media sources, when CNN puts you on the worldwide circuit, it is a mind-blowing adventure in global communications. The whole world has CNN.

We were on CNN the week after the IPO, and they reran it for the next few weeks. They'd put together this five-minute clip of Todd and me clinking champagne glasses in front of the NASDAQ screens. Everyone saw it. Everyone knew. I got a call from people all over the planet.

The punch line of the story was, "And it's run by two 24-year-old kids." This had the effect of turning theglobe.com from a news item to more of a lifestyle story, which brought it into the realm of pop culture. This in turn attracted all the consumer press. Esther was brilliant at public relations. She and her team got us into everything. And now, we were receiving endless phone calls and requests for interviews, and the entire team was inundated. During the peak, we were averaging 1,200 mentions per quarter in the U.S. print press alone. That's an average of 13 mentions per *day* without counting international exposure. Esther and her team truly brought the art of public relations to a whole new level no one had ever seen before. Often, the first question we would get from our peers in the industry was, "Who does your PR. We want the same!"

All of a sudden, we were on Fox News, the Montel Williams show, MTV, Charlie Rose. We did the morning show *Wake Up, New York*. The female interviewer said silly stuff like, "How does it feel to be worth, you know, a trillion dollars?" "Well, we're not," we'd try to say. "So," she'd continue, ignoring what we'd said, "have you gotten lots of marriage proposals. . . ."

The Montel Williams experience was great. It was an episode

about entrepreneurs. One guy had started a muffin business and built it up to $4 million in annual sales. There was another girl who developed a line of handbags made out of trash bags. Then there was Todd and me—the Internet guys. People could relate to muffins, but this Net thing was still a bit vague, so they'd made a little video clip about the site. Everyone in the audience was just, like, huh? And then Montel Williams said, "So, how much is this company worth again?" And Todd and I would try to explain it wasn't that simple, but the guy just wanted to hear us say it. So we did. "Well, it's about three quarters of a billion." "I love the ring of that," he said. "*Billion.* You boys are billionaires."

It was surreal and often achingly awkward, but it was also effective. These things would air a few times, and our audience would rocket upward. We saw shopping activity go up, traffic went up. Behold the power of the press. Between the IPO and our secondary offering in May 1999, the touch of the press was categorically positive. We had great quarters, everyone was happy, and the financial press was positive. It was exciting. The pieces varied, but they often made us look intelligent, and the stories were often flattering.

Talk about brief honeymoons. There were two groups that began the negative tide. The first one is called *Silicon Alley Reporter,* a small local rag run by a guy called Jason McCabe Calacanis. Jason had got along with us superwell before our IPO. In fact, he seemed to love us, and we did several pleasant interviews. When we had company parties, he was invited.

Then, the day we went public, the first story that came from him was practically, "Oh, these guys are a scam." Now thank God he has a small readership, but the effect was instructive. This was a major lesson for our team that we would have to be real careful. It was clear that people were going to turn on us, and we'd have to make decisions about who we talked to and who we didn't.

The other guy that started relentlessly bashing us was James Cramer of TheStreet.com. Cramer never had anything positive to say about us. His mantra was theglobe.com is wildly overvalued. Of course, look at TheStreet.com, which is nothing more than a tiny subscription-based online magazine with weak circulation that's losing massive amounts of money, and just because it's calling itself an Internet company, it's trading to massive multiples.

Now, Cramer had never met us, and he'd never interviewed us, but he had everything to say about us, portraying me and Todd as two little jerks who had absolutely no experience. How do you fight something like that? He's all over TV. This despite the fact that theglobe.com now had an audience of 15 million users. If we wanted to, we could have gone and done some bashing ourselves. CBS *Market-Watch* would have killed to film us bashing The Street, but we never did. That's stupid and small-time. We didn't want to do that. (Still, I'd be lying if I didn't say how satisfying it felt to watch TheStreet.com's stock get crushed.)

Nevertheless, despite the overwhelming positive press, the negative was out there, and it began to take on a life of its own. People had a short attention span, and when they were once fed something nasty, it was hard to convince them later they might actually like it. By loudly singling out one company—theglobe.com—Cramer created a snowball effect. Any writer considering a positive story had to worry that it would look too soft. It was amazing to us that of all the many good reporters out there, just a few bad ones could steal the limelight.

Here's a bit more context to understand Cramer's perspective. Theglobe.com went public and shot up 1,000 percent. We came down but then worked our way back up by proving our quarters and beating earnings. "Overvalued!" Cramer says. Meanwhile, TheStreet.com went public, went up 300 percent, traded at a billion-dollar market cap on zero revenues. (And let's just ignore that Yahoo, with its $100 million in revenues, was valued at $40 billion.) He must've thought, *We'll ignore the overvaluation of every Internet company except theglobe.com.* Cramer didn't just write that we were overvalued, and here's what's wrong with the principles of valuation. He was writing that theglobe.com is ludicrous because it's run by young management. Imagine! An Internet company at the dawn of the millennium, and it's run by two 24 year olds?

> > >

Now this happened sporadically in those first six months. By far and large, most of the stories were still of the pop-cultural sensation variety. We did a photo shoot for *Smart Money* magazine. They shot Todd and me in our Globe T-shirts, running down a hallway and jumping in the air. They said they wanted a shot of us in-flight. Seemed cool enough.

However, they took the shot with some sort of fish-eye lens, which makes my head look distorted. And the story is "Todd and Steph jumping for cash!"—totally sensational. We looked like smiling idiots just begging for a punch in the face. And I wanted to punch myself in the face, too—it was that cartoonish. There's nothing like the dawning feeling that people are starting to use you as whipping boys. We didn't know the half of it.

After the IPO, we did press all over the country. During one of many trips to the West Coast, we went to Los Angeles to meet with a *Los Angeles Times* writer named Jonathan Weber (some of you may recognize his name). Weber's working in this huge office with tiny cubicles everywhere, and this little guy is stuffed behind an old Mac.

So we're talking about theglobe.com (he'd wanted to meet with us), and this guy just looks totally nonplussed. His expression is like, "Yeah, okay. Right." There's no reaction out of him. The more exciting our story, the more he lulls his head like Homer Simpson. He's clearly thinking about something else while he's looking at us. And for the few moments when he was engaged, he was fairly critical of our business, asking very probing questions, tougher questions than most people get in interviews.

On the way back, Todd and I yelled at Esther. "We've really got to get better at screening these stories. This guy's probably going to write a horrible story on us." We were so pissed. Then a month goes by, and all of a sudden, this huge *Los Angeles Times* story comes out and it is superpositive, hitting on all key elements of our business. The piece gets picked up in *The Washington Post* and then runs in *The Boston Globe*. Thank you, Jonathan Weber.

Shortly thereafter, Weber mentioned to us that he's starting up a magazine on the industry (just a magazine, not an Internet business). A few months later, he started the *Industry Standard*. By then, we'd met with him a few times and had developed what we thought was a great relationship with him.

After starting the mag, Weber came to us and said he wanted to do a story on theglobe.com. "Come on," he said, "we'll do an interview with you guys. We'll set the whole thing up." Since we had this relationship, we agreed to let him put one of his reporters on us. And so, for three months, we did interviews with this one particular writer.

The writer came to New York to interview us. When we went on a trip to San Francisco, we met with her. She did phone interviews with us. It went on for so long. We actually thought the story was never going to happen because months had passed.

Then, apropos of nothing, the piece runs. And lo and behold, we're on the cover, smiling like hucksters behind a cover line that says, "The Selling of theglobe.com." The piece is about how Todd and I are selling ourselves as teen idols rather than businessmen.

When I saw the cover, my first reaction was, "That can't be good." My heart was pounding. Whenever a story we did came out, I'd be nervous and scared that some quote would get twisted around. Todd was always critical of how I spoke my mind so openly to the press. Therefore, I'd learned that the best interview format is doing it live. As much as live television seems scary, you learn they can't re-edit your comments out of context, and Todd and I had developed a knack for doing things live. Now, as I flipped through the pages, I saw comments attributed to us that could have been perceived as racist. It wasn't good.

The article actually wasn't as bashing as the things James Cramer would write, but it totally belittled everything we'd been building and representing. The end result was that it became one of those little shots in the face that started a snowball effect downward.

From then on, getting ambushed in the press was a regular occurrence. We'd always be getting calls from Mike or a friend that began, "Did you see the story?" All of a sudden, I would drop everything I was doing and try to control my breathing.

> > >

Through all this, we were laying the groundwork for a secondary offering. One of the last days before closing our offering, Alan Greenspan issued his infamous proclamation about Internet mania. "This is getting silly," he said. "You people have to stop. We're raising interest rates."

Our stock just dropped. It had dropped before, but this time things were a bit more complicated. When you gear up for a secondary offering, you're trying to raise new money. If your stock keeps dropping, it screws up your whole offering. It means you must sell twice as many shares to raise the same amount of money. Once again, we ended up raising half as much cash as we'd intended. Instead of selling 8 million shares at $40, we only managed 6.9 million at $20. That was still nothing to scoff at because we now had another $140 million, which put us ahead of most of our competition.

The press didn't miss a beat. There was a huge story in the *New York Observer*. This time, the gist was, "Globe management plunders Globe financial assets." They said Mike had cashed out and left everyone hanging. (Actually, Mike had decided he was going to sell 20 percent of his holdings during the secondary offering. Todd and I had decided to sell 5 percent. We'd been locked in for so long, we'd jumped—carefully—at our first chance to taste a little of our own profits.) But the article was the most salacious, attacking, scathing story about us I'd ever seen. It essentially said, "How *dare* they make money in the secondary offering? Shame on them for raising money and putting some in their pockets."

Of course, that was picked up by the infamous Steve Frank, a *Wall Street Journal* reporter at CNBC. And then, once again, comes TheStreet's James Cramer. Shame on the boys from theglobe.com, cashing out all that money! Remember, Mike had only taken out 20 percent, but still kept 80 percent of his holdings. Moreover, Todd and I had only cashed out about $1 million each. My God, think about the number of entrepreneurs who deal in the billions. How could they possibly pick on us when there were so many other Net companies, including TheStreet.com, that were overvalued with their founders minting money?

At the time, one thing that made this negative press tolerable was the fact that CNN was in the process of doing this huge documentary on us. Actually, Lou Dobbs had already done a general overview documentary about the craze of theglobe.com ("And how old are the founders? Twenty-four years old!"). But now, Jan Hopkins was preparing something for CNN *Movers*. *Movers* is all about people, old and young, and their great ideas that are moving and shaking.

Given the context, it was hard to imagine we were getting into anything but a positive story. So we cooperated. They wanted to film Todd and me everywhere. They really wanted to follow us around, get into our personal lives. I remember somebody saying, "Guys, let's make this well rounded. Let's see who you are as *people*."

Now, in the course of running the company and taking on the mantle of coexecutives, Todd and I had essentially been forced to live dual lives. We had to be the public face of the company. One face was the wise old businesslike CEO with no real personal life: the other was 25-year-old guy with boundless energy. So, I told them, "Screw it. If you're going to follow my life, that means out to dinner and onto the clubs. You want to do that?" And they were like, "Yes!" So that, God forgive me, was what we did.

This is where things got interesting. For Todd's story, they follow him out to the Hamptons, where he's playing badminton and hanging around at a barbecue. From there, the story cuts straight to Steph, the European boy, all dressed up in black for full-out clubbing. I had on some of these cheap, plastic pants. Todd, in what looked like a hippie commune, and me in my black, plastic pants. It was the funniest contrast and *way* overdone.

At any rate, they were filming me at home—I'd let them into my house—and a couple things happened. They were filming some B-roll, off-camera stuff, and one interviewer asked me, "So, what's it like being rich? Are you living it up?" With more than a little sarcasm, I replied, "Oh, yeah. I'm ready to live a disgusting and frivolous lifestyle."

Now this was off camera. The cameraman was literally setting up. And I, of course, was just joking, a point I reinforced by then saying, "No, no, I'm just kidding." I proceeded to tell for the eight-hundredth time that it's not at all like that, my lifestyle hasn't changed a bit. If only I wasn't so boring.

Of course, what ended up happening was that they lifted that specific quote, "I'm ready to live a disgusting and frivolous lifestyle" and then superimposed it onto a scene where you see me, on camera, right in the middle of the CNN piece.

As you might suspect, Todd was horrified when the tape aired. "Steph, why would you say that?" I had to try and explain, but it was of course extremely unbelievable that it was an off-the-cuff joke before we started. I managed to convince him, but the thing that most troubled me was that heretofore I'd have to forever put a clamp on my lips. I'd always been so open, and I liked speaking my mind. This was one of the bigger personality differences that Todd and I had discovered over the years. Whereas I like to say things exactly the way I see them (which can often be in a brutally honest and direct manner), Todd is quite puritanical, often interpreting and explaining things in a much more palatable and politically correct manner. Nevertheless, that's the lesson I learned at the time. As CEO of a public company, you've got to be very careful with what you say. (Until now, of course.)

CNN *Movers: The Story of theglobe.com* came out in July 1999. It was a half hour documentary, and it aired worldwide in multiple rotations. A lot of people saw it. The fact is that it was a great story. Anyone who watches it tends to walk away with this amazing picture of these two kids, and this was one of the first big documentaries they had done on the Internet. Overall, it was very positive.

Still, in the usual sort of way, the negative seemed to overpower the positive. The story quickly became fodder in the Yahoo message boards. It became sort of a running joke—Steph dancing in his plastic pants.

Suddenly, my pants were the reason why Greenspan came out with his comments and why Internet stocks were plummeting. It's Steph's fault. The comments on the message boards would be scathing, and of course, all our employees read those same boards. It was a total cesspool. Blasphemous.

And it got worse. We'd read things on the message boards like, "Those guys have got no clue what they're doing." "They're probably off gallivanting in their private jet." This created a vicious circle. Steve Frank on CNBC would be inspired to do another hatchet job on us. And to make a point, he got a quote from an analyst at Jupiter Communication. The analyst at Jupiter Communication would say, "Well, I don't know about you, but if you've gone on the Yahoo message boards, investors don't seem to have many positive things to say about those guys from theglobe.com." To me, using a message board in that way is no different than the FBI sourcing *The Enquirer* for hard evidence.

What's most amazing is that of the 1,200 press mentions per quarter, 75 percent were still neutral-to-positive (according to an outside firm that tracks press mentions). Consumer press, in particular, loved our story and found it inspirational. Todd and I were invited onto talk shows and as guest speakers at universities such as Harvard, MIT, and the University of Lausanne, as well as to conferences like the Industry Standard and the prestigious Connecticut Forum. We even won the 1999 Ernst & Young Entrepreneur of the Year award. People loved hearing the story as much as Todd and I enjoyed sharing it. Public speaking was really our thing. In fact, we did it so often and with such ease and enthusiasm that our presentations ran as smoothly as a scripted show. People would often approach us at the end of our talk and ask, "Can I get a copy of your script?" Of course, there was no script. Each presentation was always unrehearsed and natural, exactly the way Todd and I liked it.

Despite the largely positive press, the fraction that was negative was the U.S. financial press, and it felt a lot louder. During all of 1999 and through the first couple months of 2000, while all the new Internet IPOs kept rocketing and rocketing—EToys, $12 billion; Yahoo, up to $120 billion—we were one of the only Internet stocks that kept dropping and dropping (despite the fact that we were actually growing in business).

Why did our stock drop? Simple. When we asked investors why they sold their stock, the reason was always, "Well, you know, there's this general negative feeling about you guys and how overvalued you are." What else could anyone say? Our revenues were climbing, we were beating earnings, and we were doing all the things everybody does to beat the competition.

But negative press, especially on Wall Street, spooks people—it makes them sell. And it so happened that most of the buyers who'd blown our stock up 1,000 percent were the day traders. The institutions, the big wise, savvy investors with their own analysts? They were the ones who got in on our IPO, made 1,000 percent, and got out, leaving behind all the poor schmucks who didn't know what they were doing. The very people who Greenspan warned to avoid risky Internet trades were the same people who read the press. At the first negative sound bite, they sold.

This created a real cycle of problems in terms of building our shareholder base. We didn't have many institutional holders, and as any wise financier knows, Microsoft and all those major players have vast, vast VC, institutions, and other companies holding huge blocks of Microsoft stock. When bad comments come out and the stock drops, the pros don't necessarily sell. They hold it, weather the storm, and look at the long run.

Ultimately, Todd and I scaled down the amount of press we did in the fall. When people shove you in the trash, there's not much you can do to dig your way out. It would take a miracle, and we'd already had one.

That's one more than most people usually get.

11

THE DOWNWARD SPIRAL PART I

the slow tumble

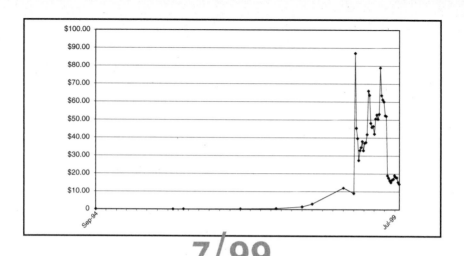

7/99

STOCK PRICE
(private company)

One thing no one ever prepares you for in the running of a public company is shareholder resentment.

I'm not talking about the big institutional investors who made a killing in Net stocks only to go on and lose money. They have resources; they work with other people's money. For them, what happened to our stock was all part of the practice of managing funds for hundreds of years. You lose some, you win some.

I'm talking about the little investors, the individuals who have to close their account at the end of the day. These people are often playing Russian roulette with their life savings. That's hard-earned money they've decided to gamble away. But individuals never see it as gambling. To them, it's calculated moneymaking.

As our stock began to fall, a Greek chorus of accusation and outrage began to rise on the sound track of our descent.

"It's the company's fault!"

177

"Todd and Steph, they should be fired!"

"They should be killed!"

"They should be lynched!"

Nice.

Some of the comments would simply be belittling, as in, "I'm sure Todd and Steph had their shareholder meeting and handed out milk and cookies to everyone. Milk and Chips Ahoy, saying, 'Everybody, let's celebrate!' "

It was hard to believe a discussion like this amongst real people could become so disgusting. Talk about the effect of anonymity on the Internet. From then on, you could forget about unbiased new traders. Any potential investors who were looking for a useful tip would suddenly be subjected to a barrage of, "You want to invest in those faggot CEOs? Don't do it! They're just going to jack you off and pump and dump," and all that sort of gentle stuff regarding the stock. Only a real exemplar of due diligence could ever reveal whether a stock was really worth buying or not.

But that was the power of these message boards; it was absolute. One renegade with an agenda had the power to influence hundreds of day traders. When hundreds of day traders sell your stock, it drops 10 percent in a day. When it drops 10 percent in one day, someone writes about it. When someone writes about it, another 100 shareholders sell. Now people have always loved to talk about trades, but until the Net, there was never the power to get the word out to 1,000 coshareholders so quickly. It was such a sudden development that it took the SEC quite a while to catch up and catch on.

It got worse. We began to notice that there was one particular shareholder lurking in the message boards by the user name of Larry_Hey. Ever since the secondary offering, this guy had been bad-mouthing us and he just wouldn't stop. He almost buried us, single-handedly. Whenever he went on one of his rampages, we would notice a drop in the stock that day. This, too, got worse.

It became clear that the hate-filled Mr. Hey was shorting our stock. Up until then, as sad as it sounds, Todd and I were not all that well informed in the mystery of "the short"—it just seemed like such an unethical thing to do. Who knew you could actually bet against a stock and then go out and ensure your profit by broadcasting what a lump of shit it was? (Of course, I soon came to think, to the extent that everything was overvalued on the Internet space, why didn't everyone short Internet stocks?)

Anyway, this guy kept bad-mouthing us and bad-mouthing us and making personal attacks on Todd and me. Often he would write, "Yes, I just saw Todd and Steph and Egan in their limo in New York. Looks like they are heading to one of the banks to go liquidate." Complete B.S., but someone was going to believe it.

We had no choice but to figure out how we could investigate and find out who this guy (and there were others, too) was. We called the FBI, but they wouldn't do anything. Technically, there was nothing illegal about it.

At the time, the securities laws hadn't caught up with this phenomenon yet, so people were free to post such messages without reprimand. Our own internal lawyer advised us to let it go. But I said, "No, we are not going to let it go." So we started tracking him ourselves like wily fox hunters. One of the first steps we took was to file an affidavit with Yahoo to get hostile member information. They found out what the guy's other user names were and what ISP he used. They gave us the information, and with that in hand, we were able to backtrack. What we quickly discovered was that this user had an account on our site.

Here's how we were able to track him down. Some user had set up a club on our site that was the TGLO Discussion Club, a successful group that often had hundreds of traders in it. Larry_Hey, of course, not being able to have anything less than the final word, joined the club on our site.

That was the biggest mistake he made. Through that, we were able to get into his account, find his user name and his password, his original name, confirm it was the same guy with Yahoo, and *gotcha*.

So we tracked him down and found out that he was a broker from a small firm in New Jersey. Just the schlockiest guy ever. It's amazing the stuff you can find out about a person. I found out which tennis club he belonged to and that he was subscribing to hair growth products on Drugstore.com. I must confess, for a moment, I thought about revenge. If I wanted to slimeball this guy and embarrass him, it would have been so easy.

What we ended up doing with counsel was sending a little FedEx package. We bundled together all these examples of his bad-mouthing and threw in everything else we'd found out about him. We put it in a legal envelope that said, "This is a cease and desist order . . ." We sent this package, not to Larry_Hey, but to his superiors at his office. We added a note that said, "Are you aware that your employee is doing the following . . . ?"

Within maybe 48 hours of sending those packages, Larry_Hey never wrote another word, at least not under *that* user name in the Yahoo message boards, and for that matter, that level of negativity dissipated. Still, the damage had been done. In terms of market cap, he almost definitely cost us tens of millions.

> > >

Beyond Larry_Hey, there were other individuals who caused us grief.

Shortly after our stock began its swan dive, this woman with a severe Asian accent started regularly calling in to tell us how evil we were. Here's a sample: "I lost my money on theglobe.com. F*ck you, I want you to die!"

She would leave voice mails for Todd and me, separately. She was relentless. Every morning, we'd walk in, ready to face the day, and the first thing we'd hear was, "I hate you! I hate you! I hate you! I will kill you! I will kill you! I will kill you! Invested my money in you. I will sue you! Class action lawsuit! I read this in the message boards, everybody hates the founders. They want you to die! Well, you should die!"

Then she'd call the head of our investor relations department and start sobbing. "I lost all my money! Please, please, please pay me back all my money, and I will be fine! Pay it back, pay it back, f*ck you! F*ck you!" It was heartbreaking. It was also pure lunacy.

Around this time, I started becoming seriously concerned that people would soon read about some deranged lunatic who'd murdered my doorman and me in my building. It was that type of lunacy. She was murderous. We'd just heard about a day trader who'd gone berserk in Atlanta and shot his colleagues, so getting killed seemed perfectly plausible.

Todd and I would laugh—she had this ridiculously thick cartoon accent—but it was a nervous laugh. We thought about security. "I'd like an officer around the clock, please." In truth, it was scary as hell. And it went on for *six* months. Over and over, in dozens of voice mails.

We never did hire protection, but the thought repeatedly crossed my mind.

The thought mostly crossed my mind at night. This was a season when I especially didn't sleep much. Pretty soon I'd be having nightmares that ended with me awake in a cold sweat, gasping for air.

12
THE DOWNWARD SPIRAL PART II
my dad

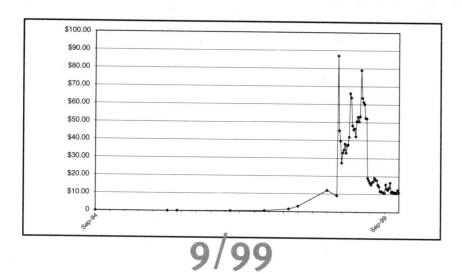

9/99

STOCK PRICE
(private company)

By the fall of 1999, Todd and I had been running the company for over five years, and the only vacation time we'd ever taken was one week during Christmas.

In September 1999, shortly after the completion of our secondary offering, Jenn and I decided to take a trip. This was particularly meaningful to me because it would be the first time I was returning to the south of France to my grandparents' house, the place where I'd summered as a teenager.

When I was 13, after spending a wonderfully isolated two weeks in France, my family and I packed up the car, planning to drive the 600 km up through most of France on our way back to Switzerland. That particular summer, things did not go exactly according to plan.

It was a warm August morning, and we had woke up extra early to pack my dad's Audi 200 turbo full of luggage. It was going to be a long and cramped journey with my dad and Monica in the front,

185

Maddy, Berthy (our 70-year-old nanny), and me in the back, and Eric and Sophie (my little brother and sister) sleeping in the rear. After a hearty breakfast and a sad good-bye with our grandparents, we all stuffed ourselves in the car and started on our merry way.

The morning quickly grew hot, and the music dad played was especially annoying. I believe it was Henri Des, a musician known for his nursery music for little infants. Dad obviously hadn't noticed that we had all aged by 10 years since he bought those tapes. Sometime around noon we stopped at a rest area for a cheap, disgusting lunch of prefab highway food.

Meanwhile, dad pulled the car up to a gas station and felt the usual urge, after being duped by the gas station attendant, that yes indeed, changing all four tires on the car was a brilliant idea. By the time we all came back from lunch, the car was sporting four new tires and a gas tank filled to the brim.

When we climbed back in the car, it was boiling hot on the black leather seats. As the A/C was cranked to the max, we pulled out of the rest area and started cruising down the four-lane highway.

Soon after leaving, Maddy mentions something to dad and Monica about the car smelling like gasoline. As usual, I chose to ignore my sister until two minutes later I started noticing the stench myself. Before I could say anything, I saw black smoke starting to seep out of the rear air-conditioning unit. Suddenly, Monica opens the passenger door for a brief instant and slams it shut again. "Yves, the front tire is on fire. Stop the car!" As the smoke got thicker and started spewing out the A/C faster, I heard Monica yell again at dad to hit the brakes. There was just one problem, as he explained to Monica through clenched teeth, "We don't *have* any brakes!"

We all were screaming. For some unknown reason, I decided to try to take a deep breath and see what it felt like to inhale the smoke. Was it really that bad? Answer: I choked before I had time to close my mouth. Dad screamed at us to open our windows. We did so, only to find all the smoke from outside the car pouring right back in.

We immediately shut them again. I noticed dad switch the ignition off and start pulling on the hand brake, but of course it was useless at that speed. He couldn't even see anymore. He opened his window again and leaned halfway out the car, past the flames. Slowly, he steered the car from the fourth lane into the third, and then the second, first, all the while dodging the other cars and looking for a soft shoulder.

Moments later, the car was on a side road, but still rolling. Dad pulled on the hand brake harder and harder. I heard screams, "Get out! Get out!" Within seconds, I was out of air and ready to pass out. With the reflexes of a mongoose, I opened the door and saw that we were still rolling and oriented myself. Right as I did so, a wall of flame surged from underneath the door. I stuck my legs through it, jumped, and ran. I must have run 50 meters without looking back. Through singed eyelids, tears were streaming down my face. I looked back terrified. The car had stopped and was completely engulfed in flames. I saw some movement in the rear seats and was sure it was my five-year-old brother Eric burning to death with his little fingers gesturing to say good-bye.

Seconds later, I saw my dad running around the back of the car, opening the hatch and grabbing everything he could, the rest of my family watching from a distance. His briefcase and a few other items are all he managed to grab. The rest stayed and burned. I found out moments later that after I had jumped out, Maddy opened her side of the car, grabbed Eric from the back, and threw him out the door; he landed straight on his nose (which would become the first of six times in his life Eric would fracture his nose). She then grabbed my little sister Sophie and ran out of the car with her. Berthy, who wasn't so fast, tried to get out after me, but she was too slow to emerge through the wall of flames so she turned around and crawled out behind Maddy. Monica and dad ran around and made sure we were all out.

We all backed away from the car and watched as it burned like a huge torch. It kept burning until the fire brigade showed up. In the end, there was nothing left but a wire frame of what was once a car, sitting in the middle of a puddle of molten metal. In what used to be the trunk, we found hideously twisted tennis rackets, charred bags, half-burned passports, and some of Monica's jewelry.

I like to think this wasn't the reason I had never returned to the south of France, but subconsciously, this must have affected me more deeply than I'd realized. Moreover, this accident was about as emotional as things got between me and dad. But it wasn't to be the last.

Fast-forward again to 1999. I was going back to France with Jenn as a grown man, and it would be the first time that she would actually spend time with my dad's side of the family, including my grandparents. I knew that my grandparents were certainly nervous that I was seriously involved again—especially with an American woman, a girl from Kentucky who'd grown up to be a New York model. My grandparents had all these apprehensions about what sort of a life I was leading.

It was a very exciting time. With my dad there, I was nervous about having to relive a lot of my childhood emotions in front of Jenn. Though I loved the beauty of southern France, I also remembered the crushing feeling of isolation. Our house is on a cliff, perched on the lip of a treacherous 200-foot drop to the ocean. It's absolutely beautiful but completely unforgiving.

> > >

Close your eyes. Imagine escaping from the stress of your job and waking up late in the day to the sound of the ocean and the breeze outside. Now imagine what simplicity looks like. Old wooden bed, little wooden chair, that's it. You walk into my old little bedroom, and there's this giant wooden closet that has sat there for 50 years. All day long, there's the sound of crickets. We'd have a breakfast, a late lunch, and take an afternoon siesta.

What a contrast from Manhattan and our fibrillating stock price. To make it even better, things were going famously with my dad. We went swimming and sailing every day. It was a peaceful time, especially between father and son.

There was just one nagging problem: He had this constant lower back pain. He had no idea what it was. He thought it might be a slipped disk, but whatever the cause, it was beginning to hurt a lot.

That didn't stop him from enjoying the food and the cheese and entertaining the guests my family would invite for a visit. I remember one day, Jenn, my stepmother Monica, and I took the car and drove to the local market. My dad decided to take a long walk from the house; it must have been a good five miles.

Now, my dad is a real mountaineer. He's hiked up the Himalayas. He's also a heavyset guy, about 200 pounds. He's the kind of guy who's been a businessman most of his life and so never got enough regular exercise other than sailing across the Atlantic or doing some heavy-duty weekend warfare. This was his usual attempt at that. He showed up after his hike, sweaty and exhausted. He was in a lot of pain. "My damn back," he said. But then he shrugged it off.

> > >

When the vacation ended, I returned to New York with Jenn, fully recharged and refreshed. Three weeks passed, it's late September, and all hell was breaking loose with theglobe.com—the crazy shareholders, the libelous postings, the hemorrhaging stock price. Toward the end of a working Thursday, around 4:00, I received a phone call from Monica.

Now, just two days before, my father had called to say hi and to tell me that he was going in for a checkup the next day. Uncharacteristically, it almost sounded like he was a little scared about going to see a doctor. I was really touched. "I want you to know, Steph," he said, "how much I love you." He hadn't said those words, ever. "Okay, dad, stop being such a worrywart. It's fine," I teased him.

But then Monica called and said, "Well, Steph, your dad went in for a checkup, and things are a lot worse than we expected. He's been in the hospital in surgery now for six or seven hours."

It turned out they found cancer, and that it had already spread all over his body. Before I could form a thought, she continued, "They're trying to make a decision about how much of his body to cut out because it seems to have spread to a lot of different organs, and it seems to be very serious."

I remember exactly how hard it was to comprehend what she was saying. I'd just seen him. He was fine. I was sure it was going to be okay.

Then, later the next day, I got an update from my mother in London. He was now in intensive care; they stopped operating, but things were far worse than they'd first expected. The family had consulted with one of our longtime friends, Jack Hildebrand, a good general practitioner in California who had been a family friend for 30 years.

Jack talked with the doctors in Switzerland to get a better understanding of what was going on; then he'd translate to my mom and Monica. The upshot was advanced pancreatic cancer, which was known to have a near 100 percent mortality rate within five years. They had to make the decision whether to operate in the first place because when something has spread that much, they could just as well kill you on the operating table. The Swiss physician was one of those doctors willing to take risks, and he'd studied this procedure quite a bit. Jack felt that if he hadn't operated as much as he did, my dad would have been dead within two months. Jack also felt that he was far from out of the woods. When I heard all of this, my reaction was, "What are you talking about? How could he be dead within a couple months?" I remained in complete denial.

The question became whether he'd survive the surgery, which there'd be more of. They'd have to reconstruct his stomach because so much would be removed. He was on life support by then and had been semi-unconscious for a few days.

Then, the day after, my mom called again in the early afternoon. The office was luckily empty. Todd was in California with Mike, meeting with a potential suitor. My mom was scared. Despite the divorce, they've always gotten along really well and she's always loved my dad.

She said, "Steph, do you understand how bad this is?"

Automatically, I said, "Yeah, they had to operate, but everything is going to be fine."

"Well, it's not that simple, Steph," she said. "Your dad is really sick." She paused. "The chances of his survival are slim to none."

As if nothing had sunk in, I responded, "Okay, I understand that, mom, but everything is going to be *fine.*"

"Steph," she said, "your dad may only have a few months left to live."

I got up and shut the door to the office, which is soundproof because Todd and I used to scream at each other. I got back on the phone, and I could barely get the words out. "What are you saying?"

For the first time, I was listening to what she was saying. My mother had tears in her voice, and I just remember this lump building in my throat and the emptiness in my stomach.

The shock wasn't so much the illness, but the cruel, entirely implausible surprise of the thing. I always felt I'd have my whole life to get to know my dad. It was shocking me and pissing me off at the same time that I might not have the chance to listen and speak with him as I began my own family, continued my own business ventures. That I wasn't going to be able to outsmart my dad at every conversation and keep him up-to-date on policy and business.

None of that would happen. It would all just vanish. I'd be left with my grandfather, who's even more closeminded, and . . . our stock was still sinking; I'd promised my dad that I'd be damned if I left theglobe.com before the stock was up to $100. Now he was apparently leaving, and no contingency for that.

After I got off the phone with my mother, it was around 2:00 in the afternoon. Since I couldn't think straight, I got out of there and just wandered around for hours. I went home, took a hot shower, and just sat down right there under the hot water, crying. I felt this huge sinking sensation. Nothing made sense to me anymore.

That evening I booked a ticket to Switzerland.

I left the next day, a Friday afternoon. I hopped on the plane looking like a total bum. Of course, I hadn't slept. I hadn't even shaved.

I arrived at 9 A.M. in Switzerland, now having not slept for two consecutive nights. I looked like a day hiker who's been lost in the Alps for three days. I went straight from the airport to the hospital. Monica and my stepbrother and stepsister were there already, waiting for me.

Before the nurse on duty let us in, she mentioned that my father was still on severe medication and that he'd be in and out of consciousness the whole time. As I listened, my stomach twisted in knots. I'd been in the hospital often enough for my own digestive treatments that the smell, that antiseptic smell, was making me nauseous. The smell also reminded me that this was the same Swiss hospital where I had my appendix taken out.

> > >

He didn't look like my father. He was lying on his back with tubes going into his stomach, his arm, and up his nose. They'd cut so much out of him. It turned out that they had to open his leg and take out nerves and veins to reconstruct the canal system in his stomach. He looked like a hunched old man. What was most mind-blowing was my dad had always been such a larger-than-life character, a powerful figure. He knew business and politics, and on those matters, he was a lion. Now he looked so thin and weak. He'd always been this guy that I feared, especially physically, because I knew that if he lost his temper, he might hit someone. Now the skin sagged from his neck. From not having eaten in five days, his weight plummeted. He was yellow-pale; his skin seemed to be dying.

Monica told me to sit beside him. He'd been asking to see me. He sort of looked over, but his eyes weren't really focusing, they were wobbling from side to side. His mouth was bone-dry. I took his hand, which felt lifeless and weak, but it was still warm, thank God.

My dad said to me (in French), "You know, Steph, I think I've been dealt a really poor hand." Then he was crying. "I wanted . . . I have no time now to say anything to anyone." I told him everything was going to be fine, and tears welled up in my eyes. My family was sitting at the end of the bed, completely quiet. Dad said, "There are so many things we need to work out. I have so many business issues that are unresolved, that we need to wind down. I need your help, Steph. There are these businesses in the States."

He started going through all of them. My father had always been a businessman, and once again, everything was coming out business, business, business. And I said, "Dad, let's not talk about this right now." But he kept going. "Steph, there's Icon in California. There is this medical company I told you about. And there's this one in Boston, and one in France, and we need your help." All the while, he was crying, and he couldn't stop.

Then, just as quickly, he calmed down and immediately dozed off. I mean, just completely dozed off. We stepped out, and the nurses went in to look after him.

As I waited outside, I thought about the irony of my dad's role in theglobe.com. After meeting the whole thing with skepticism (but never negativity), he became a big believer. He'd invested in an online medical company in Atlanta, and that company had merged with WebMD, and then WebMD merged with Healtheon. Suddenly, my dad was an investor in one of the biggest healthcare companies online. He'd become a massive convert. Even so, he always told me it was all a massive bubble that was going to burst; it was just a question of time. He was the first person that told me, long before anyone else, that people should absolutely not believe the hype.

As the business grew, my dad would always give me advice about how we weren't being handled correctly, whether I liked it or not. I'd say, "Yes, dad, thank you. I have already heard this a trillion times," but he was always right and he always had to have the last word. The Net became the one place where he'd ultimately defer to *my* opinion—my only oedipal triumph since the divorce, and I went with mom.

I suppose my father first became a Net convert when he heard that Geocities received a $227 million valuation, which enabled it to get all that mezzanine financing *before* it went public. The day my dad heard that, he was like, "Damn, you guys are worth $200 million, too!" I remember saying, "Dad, thank you!" Just six months earlier he had said, "How the hell do you guys come up with these valuations? I mean, $20 million for theglobe.com seems very steep. You are not profitable." After GeoCities, he finally saw the light. After *many* arguments.

Now, as I sat there, my dad essentially on his deathbed, I had to smile. I was struck by the sudden realization that we had more in common than I could have ever imagined.

I told Monica that I'd be happy to tell dad that I'd take care of everything for him, but I recommended that it would be better to hire someone to manage dad's assets because I didn't know the first thing about them. Who was I to claim any knowledge about the healthcare business or the human resources business?

The prognosis was far from great. I'd met with the doctor, this tough old Swiss guy, and frankly, the sight of him made me nervous. I'd been thinking to myself, *We need to get an American doctor on this.* I said to my dad's doctor, "Well, have you consulted with any American doctors?" And he said, "The American doctors would have recommended *not* to operate. And quite frankly, I think that your father could have died right away if we hadn't."

We'd have to wait a couple of weeks to see whether he could physically heal from the wounds. If he managed to survive that, then would come the real hard part—full chemotherapy treatments and full radiation therapy, months of pumping poison through his body over and over.

The theory was that if he could survive the first year with no signs of a reoccurrence, then chances were very good that he could make it a second year and a third year.

On Sunday, I boarded the plane and headed back to New York, to the office.

First thing Monday morning, I told Todd. As strange as it sounds, my father's illness had a cathartic effect on us; it was a way for us to release all this pent up malignancy.

Suddenly, nothing about work mattered to me in the same way. I didn't even want to talk about it. Meanwhile, I didn't want to tell anyone at the office about my dad, it was just too tiring to get into. But I still had to keep a good face. I had to get in front of the camera to meet press. I also had to keep Mike apprised of how the quarter was shaping up and how everything was going.

Thank God there were two of us. Behind closed doors, Todd was the crutch I had to lean on. This was the time when we were being buried by the message boards and watching the stock sink. I dreamed that we could rewind and unbuy Azazz and unbuy what-ever other junk we'd gotten stuck with. It was all just a mess. We had weak ad sales. E-commerce had not panned out. The guys in Seattle were just lumps of coal. I started to ask myself, *Why are we doing this?*

Todd and I made a pact the day we started this business that we will do this only so long as we're having fun. We looked each other in the eye and said, "Let's not turn this into some silly little saying that just vanishes. We will only do this if we love it every day." Now we were falling out of love.

We knew we were going to be short revenues in the third quarter, for the first time in the company history. The cancer that had been growing in theglobe.com was finally catching up with us. Todd and I were having our first serious talk about whether there was anyway we would be able to survive.

Thus began the next major pull of the downward spiral.

13

THE DOWNWARD SPIRAL PART III

mutiny and the decision

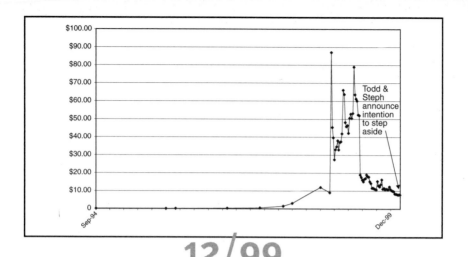

12/99

STOCK PRICE
(private company)

W e held our secondary offering during the two weeks that came to an end on May 19, 1999. Those days will live in infamy for me as the true beginning of the end.

Obviously, there were hundreds of factors that fed into this inexorable finish—the libelous message boards and vitriolic bad press, not to mention my emotional state regarding my father's health—but the key ingredient that started it was a cumulative negativity that became endemic and incurable, and how that negative perception became a reality in the form of a plunging stock price.

That, for me, remained the most frustrating part of this whole ordeal because revenues were climbing and we had beaten every quarter right out of the gate. Our dropping stock price had nothing to do with how the company was performing.

> > >

For a while, Todd and I had the fighting spirit. "Oh, well, *fine*, we'll prove everybody wrong." But what starts to happen is that you reach critical mass and find yourself pushing a bigger and bigger boulder uphill. It eventually gets so big that it actually starts to push you backward.

We did everything to ignore the daily stock price and just focus on the business. But even when you don't seek out the information, someone comes in and tells you your stock price or there's yet another article about its drop. All day long, your employees (and you) are measuring the company's success—and their own personal success—based on where the price is that afternoon. The more the stock price dropped, of course, the more depressed everyone in the company would become.

Look at Microsoft. For the first time in its history, it dropped 50 percent, and as a result they suffered record numbers of employees leaving, senior managers, everything. Clearly, when people have a perception that they can't really make money anymore, that they cannot ever get the stock back enough to make money, it cuts in such a deep way, they're willing to give up a job they love, even a well-paid cash position. They'd rather jump onto something else, even if there's a bigger chance that that company will fail.

Frequently, it did happen that way. We'd have employees leave for what they thought was their dream job. A month later, we'd hear they were fired or quit, or the company they'd thought so highly of had gone under. Very frequently, they came back. One of our top database programmers left to do high-tech video. Within a month, he quit that and asked for his old job back. We gave it to him.

Still, desperate negativity starts to crush you. Inevitably, your clients start to hear it. Clients read. All of a sudden, advertisers start to pull their accounts; new clients are a lot less interested. Now their first question isn't, "Hey, what's your demo?" It's, "Hey, so how long are you guys going to be in business?" We'd have to tell people, "We have enough cash to last at least another two years. We are in the top 20 percent of publicly traded Internet companies. There is nothing to worry about." Nevertheless, the fact that you had to have these conversations was a bad sign.

> > >

Let me summarize how we looked by mid-1999. By the secondary offering, theglobe.com had gone through some major restructuring, much of it based on how the competition had grown. Geocities had been bought by Yahoo; Tripod was snapped up by Lycos. In effect, our toughest competitors were removed as brands.

We'd grown from 5 or 6 million users at the IPO to 15 million users worldwide after the secondary offering. Media Metrics ranked us the 34th biggest site in the world, and that included measurements from every major country. We were very proud of what we had accomplished.

But by then, users had more choices. They could go to Yahoo where they could get absolutely everything, or they could go to theglobe.com where they could get much less than at Yahoo.

We changed from being a pure community to trying to become a portal. We'd dabbled with being an e-commerce company. We'd suffered greatly in the unfocused search for what was seen as the next big thing.

In June 1999, we decided we would need a massive restructuring. On the heels of the secondary offering in which we had raised another $140 million, we brought in all the key managers from around the world, from the United Kingdom, from Seattle, from wherever. It was amazing to see the great talent we had managed to attract over the years. Between the IPO and the continuous press, our brand had become very well known, and our company seemed hip, truly alive. In turn, this attracted many pioneering, creative, hardworking employees, most of whom are still with us today. We brought them in and had a major meeting. We decided to restructure the company to revolve more clearly around the products. We would be product focused (clubs, home pages, games), and everything would be built upon that.

One of the products that had just emerged was e-mail clubs, a product that I personally really loved. I truly believed that e-mail clubs were the sequel to community. So we implemented the changes, launched the clubs, a new home-page builder and a whole new site design. Employees became very positive. For once, we felt on the cutting edge with our products. But on the flip side, we were being crushed by a slowdown in sales—our sales force was not mature enough and quickly became overburdened. It was our weakest link. We didn't quite realize it at first. We had gone from just $0.75 million in sales in 1997 to $18.6 million in revenues in 1999. We had this huge ramp-up and much of that we attributed to our energetic sales force, which numbered in the low thirties by this time.

Our internal goal for 1999 was to hit $25 million in sales. The analysts knew we were supposed to do about $18 million, and when we came in at $18.6, we'd technically beat the analysts' numbers, which was fantastic.

But the reality was that after we went public, we kept missing every *internal* goal we had set. Despite padding our numbers with each additional acquisition, sales just couldn't stay ahead of the curve.

As we headed into the third quarter of 1999, suddenly, revenues were coming in way short. Todd and I were horrified. Then, in July, ad sales fell through completely. We'd been doing about $1 million and a quarter a month from ad sales alone. By the end of July, revenue had dropped to half a million.

We'd dropped $700,000 in revenues! Sales would say, "We had a bad month. We'll make up for it." And so they tried. Revenues ramped up. August jumped to a million. In September, we got up to $1 million and three quarters in sales.

But July's loss of half a million was a fatal blow. After factoring in another million we'd lost in e-commerce, we came in short of Bear Stearns's revenue estimate. We'd actually missed other analysts' estimates by about $300,000, but they'd all said, "That's fine, no problem." Our losses were low enough that—once again—we had beat their earnings-per-share figures.

Bear Stearns, on the other hand, came down with severity. Naturally, the press had a field day. James Cramer kept rerunning the story, and we were getting crushed.

> > >

Obviously, there was a lot of pressure on ad sales to produce numbers. Slowly, we began to sense a perception among members of the sales group that we were these two kids isolated in our ivory tower, running the company without knowing anything. We believed it was fueled by Will and Bryan, our two senior sales executives, who we later learned had their own agenda.

As the business models for highly valued Internet companies grew shakier in the late nineties rather than more stable, the sales group pressed to catch up, frantically trying to ramp up their advertising numbers. At the same time, it seemed like some of them had a growing sense of self-importance as their own entity, separate and distinct from the rest of the company. With the endless bashing in the press, our public reputations as CEOs were getting seriously tarnished, and the missed quarter had only made things worse. Yet management, the board, and sales *together* set the targets for internal revenue goals.

Remember the cartoon we drew of the Azazz debacle? I had a sudden, ironic flashback when I noticed that on the big white board in the sales office, someone had gone so far as to draw a little cartoon of a cliff with Will and Bryan falling off of it, presumably reinforcing the point that, in their eyes, the pressure was on them exclusively. Which was interesting, because on the outside everyone was painting Todd and me as the fall guys.

There was also pressure coming the other way, from sales back to us, for more stock options. Remember, this was still during the salad days and our stock was high. Our people were getting stock at $30 a share. Then, after the secondary offering, our stock dropped and dropped. Around the time it was $15 a share, we began hearing from a few executives in sales, "Well, thanks for the 70,000 shares, but now they're not worth anything." These demands became hard for everyone in senior management to ignore.

At the time, we thought it more important to hit our quarter than to cause disharmony with our sales team. So we caved. Our attitude for a while became, "Okay, fine, have your stock options." Obviously, the economy was exploding and all around us in New York people were comparing their options packages over drinks, packages that very soon, for many of them, would become worthless. But everyone wanted a piece of the pie, and we had a few people who continually came back to us, trying to renegotiate their options package as the price continued to drop. Todd and I were stunned by their expectations. We felt backed into a corner. They knew how much we were relying on them. But at a certain point, we simply had to say, "No more. You're playing with this stock like its monopoly money."

Suddenly, there was this systemic perception that Todd and I weren't willing to reward good performance. Then the stock dropped even further. And Todd and I had to wonder what kind of performance people expected should be rewarded. I know what you're thinking. People always ask me, "Why did you keep renegotiating?" Well, this was all happening in real time, right here, right now, *today*. Every day of a quarter represents 1.1 percent of your sales for that quarter. It would take three to six months to find replacements for anyone we let go. If we lost our top salespeople, all of a sudden we'd have to explain to The Street why we missed our revenue—not by 5 percent or by 1 cent a share—but by 20 cents a share or a massive 50 percent. When things fall apart like that you don't have time to work it out. And the analysts were looking for us to trip up.

> > >

It was unbearable, and it would get uglier. I was also dealing at the time with my dad's ordeal. What we'd soon realize was Will and Bryan were privately talking to Ed. They must have known that Ed had Mike's ear.

Fortunately, Ed's loyalty was to Todd and me. Although he was loyal to Mike in terms of being a manager, Ed was phenomenal at being an adviser to us and a buffer. There were a number of times when Todd and I were ready to blow up at Mike, and Ed would be the one saying, "Don't do that. Here is how I suggest you make things right."

I'm well aware that part of this was our fault. It was our fault that our senior management team didn't act in a stronger and more authoritative way with our own managers. Todd and I didn't have 30 years of experience managing such situations to know that you either attack it the first time it happens and do so systematically and consistently whether it's a big issue or tiny issue, or it gets out of hand down the road. But Todd and I, along with Dean and Frank, didn't necessarily deal with it aggressively enough, and this error only exacerbated the situation.

At the end of December, I went to Switzerland to see my dad.

I came back, and Todd then left on his vacation. I walked into the office on January 6 to find it half-empty and our stock down to around $10 a share and fluctuating. The energy had left the building so to speak. For a split second, sitting at my desk and listening to the silence, I had a rushing sense of foreboding. Then Dean Daniels came in to the office and explained that Will and Bryan were down in Florida, working on a business deal with Sportsline.

We'd been talking to Sportsline, one of the largest sports sites, for month after month after month. This was going to be our big, big anchor deal, the first huge company wanting to make a deal to use our community. Bryan started talking to them in the fall of 1999. The deal was finalized around late March, and it turned out to be the worst deal we made in company history. We paid out a whopping $8 million in stock with the expectation of making millions in revenue. It has probably made less than $100,000 in total revenues for us. It's been a massive loss.

So I'm back and I'm sick as a dog. Todd is skiing in Aspen, and I'm just deflated. Chronic stress has left me permanently ill. Then I get a call from Ed at Mike's Florida office.

"What's up, Ed?"

Ed said, "Hey, I just want you to know that Will and Bryan have been here all morning with Mike. They're scheduled to be here all day."

"What?"

"Yeah, I didn't know if you knew or not. I just wanted to fill you in." Ed had broken out of the meeting to tell me this. He said, "I'll tell you more later."

This wasn't good. Up till this point, my relationship with Will and Bryan had been cordial—tense, but cordial, all things considered. All of which made this much more shocking. Todd was totally out of the loop. He was skiing and blissfully free; I was on my own and going out of my mind. My heart stopped, and the pit of my stomach was erupting. I called Todd and left him a voice mail (he never had his cell phone on, which just frustrated the hell out of me).

Finally, I got Mike on the phone and let him talk.

"Will and Bryan are down here," he said, "and they're giving us some valuable feedback. They think there are a lot of changes that need to be made. They think you guys are not communicating with everybody properly, and they have a list of things they think should change. Oh, and that you should step aside." Mike said that, obviously, he didn't necessarily think we should step aside, but that we needed to work on the communication problems.

I was flabbergasted that the meeting had even occurred. For a moment, I couldn't answer. I was just trembling on the phone. Trembling with rage. Finally, I said something like, "Okay, okay, *okay*. I gotta call you back."

Half an hour later, Todd called. We had a crazy David Mamet conversation:

"Guess what?"

"What?"

"No!"

"No?"

"Yes?"

"Yes!"

I told Todd the whole goddamn thing. Now, between Todd and me, I had always been the guy who's more passionate and aggressive. But Todd had changed, and so had I—and only Todd knew what was happening with my father. Seeing the cancer eat away his vitality, it became truly apparent that there was more to life than theglobe.com, but I said to Todd, "I'm thinking we should fly right down to Florida and storm in there. . . ."

Todd interrupted, "Tell Mike we're out."

"What?"

Todd was oddly calm. He was like a Zen master. "That's it," he said. "That's it. Let's go tell him we are out. We are out, we are out!"

"What do you mean out?" I said. "Do you mean we're quitting?"

"Steph," he said, and I could hear the smile forming on his face, "we are f*cking out! That's it!"

The minute I heard Todd say what until recently had been inconceivable, I knew in my heart of hearts that I was ready to step aside, that this had been too much. Todd and I had always needed to be together on all the big decisions. Over the years, we'd fought about a lot, but on this, we were in total agreement.

> > >

And so I hung up and called Mike back.

"Mike," I said, "I just want you to know Todd and I are really disappointed. We are really disappointed, and this is absolutely unacceptable." It was very quiet on the other end. I explained to Mike how upset I was that Will and Bryan had set this meeting up without our knowledge. I took a deep breath, "Mike, I just want you to know that we're out, Todd and I are resigning."

Mike started in immediately. "Now, hold on. I wouldn't be so brash. We can work this out. There is nothing to be so crazy about."

"No," I said. What I wanted to tell Mike was that I was just as pissed at him for having taken the meeting. I said, "It seems like you've really lost faith in us."

Mike said, "No, I have never lost faith in you guys." He was backtracking, but in the end it was obvious that he couldn't stop us from leaving.

After I got off the phone, Ed called. He wanted to know if it was true. I told him we were dead serious. He didn't want us to do anything brash, either. "You have a lot of shares in this company," he reminded me. "The last thing we want is some big scandal to appear in the newspapers."

"Believe me," I said, "Todd and I are not stupid. I believe in this company, and I love the company. It's heart-wrenching for me to have to let go. Don't worry," I told him, "nothing stupid is going to happen. We are going to take our time."

> > >

This all went down on Thursday, January 6, 2000. That night, Todd got on a plane and came back. He arrived Friday afternoon and came over to my place. We pulled out the vodka, and Jenn, who'd known all of this stuff from the get-go, was our personal bartender. We all had tears in our eyes, but we were also wildly excited at the same time. We held up the shot glasses and grinned. We had drink after drink after drink, giddy with laughter and freedom.

That whole weekend was a blur and all the while, I floated with excitement. I was also delusionally scared. I had no idea what was going to happen. But we had to be adamant about our decision. "We are going through with this," we told each other, "we are definitely going through with this, but we have to do a very orderly transition."

On a wintry gray morning in early January 2000, we agreed that we'd note our departure at the quarterly announcement, and that we'd put out a press release. The release would make it clear that though Todd and I were indeed stepping aside, we were going to continue as board members. We would continue, just like Bill Gates, as chief strategists. We'd also help the company transition, find a new CEO, even guarantee a new CEO before the end of the second quarter.

There were a lot of factors that fed into our decision. Will and Bryan were merely the last straw. The reality was that Todd and I were ready to go. The attempted force-out, unpleasant at first, became a good reason to exit, and there was little Mike could do to argue with us. This had been building ever since we went public, since that day we realized that this was all falling out of our control. We had designed the car and started the engine, but we were very quickly becoming passengers in our own vehicle. (We'd also learned how few CEOs are actually in absolute control of their company. Take Mike Armstrong of AT&T, a very savvy exec who had to watch his stock drop 82 percent. It was better to be the founder and then maintain control of your equity by relinquishing the reins to better trained, more experienced people.)

Todd and I used to draw these massive spirals on our blackboard—these perfectly symmetrical spirals. I called them the spirals of despair. There's nothing worse than the dawning feeling that things can actually get worse. In fact, around the time of the secondary offering, Todd and I suggested that the board seriously consider hiring a new CEO, a leader who could just take over and really push through.

The board's general reaction was, "If it ain't broke. . . ." They never believed that the company was broken. After all, we were still a half-billion-dollar enterprise, and we'd also managed to consistently beat earnings every quarter. They didn't believe there was anything wrong with Todd and me. It was just about giving us good advice and making things work. Despite this, Todd and I mentioned that we weren't against the idea of bringing in a new CEO, but they wanted us to stay.

But we'd made our decision. Life was too important.

I wanted to spend some time with my dad.

> > >

The last few months leading up to the big earnings announcement had been an emotional hellhole. Thank God I had Jenn and the comfort of lying on the couch with her while she ran her hand through my hair and listened to all this crap. I remember speaking with my mother and telling her over and over again, "All of this needs to go away!" She was tirelessly supportive, as she has always been throughout my life.

Meanwhile, our stock price had dropped from a high of $43 (postsplit) to $10 a share. We'd been in the process of courting a buyout. We'd been talking with David Wetherell at CMGI, but they backed away—partly because we had to keep renegotiating the price as their stock ran up, but largely because Wetherell seemed like an emotional basket case who couldn't make up his mind. An opinion that later seemed more substantiated by a massive *New York Times* piece about him.

All I dreamed of doing was selling the company, getting back to Switzerland, and spending time with my dad. But it just wasn't happening yet—the company was no longer fully in our control. And the press wouldn't stop slamming us. Todd and I simply weren't strong enough to take the whole thing back in hand. At the same time, we didn't know if we *wanted* to take it back in hand.

> > >

This is the point where we reached the classic crossroads. That joke sign in the Texas desert that says, "10,000 miles to Paris, 3,000 miles to Timbuktu, 7,000 miles to Tokyo"—this is exactly how Todd and I felt. We didn't know if we were pointing in the right direction or what the distances were, and we didn't have any water left in our canteen.

Once, while visiting in Switzerland and having dinner with the family, my grandmother (who doesn't exactly have 20/20 vision) looked at me across the table and said, "Steph, you look like you have put some weight on," just as I'm stuffing my face. It was mortifying. I was getting fat, *and* I was miserable.

We'd never started theglobe.com to be slaves to a stock price or to an investor community. We'd never expected to have our lives judged day in and day out by people who formed their opinions based on how much money they'd made or lost in a single afternoon.

We had a vision, and we'd gone for it. That's all that Todd and I had originally done. Obviously, when something goes too far, you can't turn back and cry for your days of innocence. Todd and I realized that the only thing we could do was change the future and take control of our personal lives.

Which, of course, is exactly what we did.

14
THE SECOND COMING

It's not about how far down below zero you go, it's about how fast you go back through zero on your way to the top.

—Anders Bergendahl

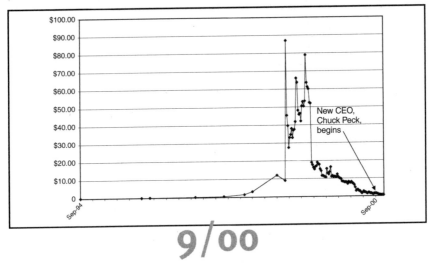

9/00

STOCK PRICE
(private company)

After Todd and I made our big decision, we had to keep our mouths closed. After all, we had a vested interest in cooperating with Mike and making sure that the cathartic thrill of our departure didn't come at the deadly expense of our stock price. Still, that didn't stop Ed from saying, "I assume you guys won't go and do something stupid like talking to the press." We had no intention of talking to the press. The plan was that Todd and I would keep our lips zipped until January 27, when we were to announce our next quarterly results.

It's not easy to keep that kind of secret. We couldn't discuss it with our employees, and I had to swear my girlfriend to secrecy. The only people who knew were our COO, Dean Daniels, and our head of communications, Esther Loewy.

January 27 was a bittersweet day. We'd just happened to be wrapping up our best quarter ever, and Todd and I were proud of those numbers. At least we were stepping aside on a good note.

Once the big news went out over the wire, we immediately held an internal meeting. Despite our silence, rumors had been flying about what was going on. Still, some people were genuinely in shock when we told them.

It wasn't easy. Of course, we couldn't tell them all the hateful things that had gone down behind the scenes. We just let people know that stepping down was the best thing for the company. We explained that Todd and I would be relinquishing day-to-day operations and that Dean would be stepping up as president. We'd continue to deal with the things that he didn't have time for. Over the next six months, we'd announce a new CEO.

After the meeting, we did the conference call with the analysts and spent five minutes placating them about our sudden departure. Then we passed over the phone. It was Dean's turn to talk. Dean gave a whole debriefing on the quarter. He did a great job. We just sat there, not saying a word.

> > >

Then we went back to our office and closed the door behind us. We gave each other a hug and wrote on the board, "It's done!" I had a little disposable camera, and we took goofy thumbs-up pictures.

I'll never forget that initial thrilling sensation of freedom, sitting in our office, the weight finally lifted. We'd been on a roller coaster that had nearly careened out of control to the point that sparks were flying, and we'd actually jumped the tracks. Now, it was done. Over the next six months, we'd work out the legal details, gradually give up the reins, look for that new CEO, and try to learn how to enjoy life again.

For the first time, we could breathe. It was like taking a huge swan dive off a cliff and landing on a silk bed. It felt so good knowing that we'd finally made this decision, an honest decision. We'd been raising this baby for six years. Now we finally let it go; someone else would be doing the diapering.

On the day of our announcement, the stock was around $9 a share (postsplit). In some vengeful reporters' eyes, the price was just another sign of our incompetence. Of course, what we couldn't have known was that two and a half months later, the massive Internet bubble would burst, and 90 percent of all Internet companies would drop 90 percent in value.

Who knows what would have happened if we'd all fallen together, as opposed to theglobe.com falling just a few months ahead of the curve. Maybe Todd and I would've stayed longer, maybe we would have been willing to put up with everything, and nobody would have been banging us constantly about our stock price. But . . . whatever.

What no one else knew at the time was that we'd entered into intense discussions with a company that wanted to buy theglobe.com. The negotiations had been going on for a couple of months.

We were talking to the publishing company E-Map Peterson. They'd been looking to implement a big Internet strategy, and they liked that we offered niche services that could work with their niche publications. (We'd also had discussions before with Tom Rogers at Primedia, Mel Karmizan at CBS, Bob Wright at NBC, and many more.) But E-Map had concerns. They could never understand why our stock had dropped so much, and this (ruinously) was always in the back of their minds.

Of course, had we been part of the entire market crapping out, they might have said, "Oh, well, good, theglobe.com is actually no different from the rest of them." But it didn't work out like that in the end, and it didn't help that Mike was pushing hard—perhaps too hard—on Todd and me for the deal. In the end, E-Map backed away completely.

> > >

As a result of the failed E-Map deal, we lost a couple of months in our search for a new CEO. And so in March 2000, Todd and I started looking in earnest.

We interviewed several candidates, all from traditional companies. We were looking for someone with the requisite amount of energy to take on something huge like this, and for someone who *wasn't* an Internet exec. We talked to one major media player who was among the top people at Random House, and several candidates of a similar caliber.

Ultimately, the man we hired was Chuck Peck, a self-described "challenge junkie" from the AICPA and Simon & Schuster who'd been a lifelong turnaround artist. Chuck had helped build New York Air with Frank Lorenzo. He'd secured $150 million in sales and overseen some 3,000 employees. He was a former marine, which clearly added a little discipline to the gig. He was a bull dog, a guy with a gift for raw pushing, and his strength was especially in sales and marketing.

Just the year before, we had moved into new cutting-edge offices down on Wall Street, and we knew that as soon as Chuck arrived he could revolutionize the organization and really get our sales moving. We knew he'd be able to gun it. He wasn't one of those toothless CEOs who overanalyzed everything and never made ends meet.

And so, on August 1, 2000, Chuck came on board while Todd and I began our gradual unwinding.

We became the backseat guys, and we tried extra hard to not be backseat drivers. One of the biggest failures many companies suffer is when their new CEOs come in only to find themselves smothered by the predecessors. We couldn't risk that kind of counterproductivity.

In January, February, and March, the market was still up. NASDAQ was holding at 5,000. Everyone was minting money left and right in different Internet investments. Meanwhile, Todd and I had all our stock in theglobe.com, which was still—slowly but surely—going down. So you can imagine how frustrating it was when everyone else celebrated, "Whoo-hoo, I've got my money in EToys, in this $10 billion company!" and "WebVan is a $20 billion company. It's just fantastic!"

Don't forget, Todd and I knew all these companies pre-IPO. We knew the people from UrbanFetch and Kozmo, which were on fire. We knew them like no one else knew them. In fact, we knew them so well that Todd and I decided to borrow money against our stock, because at the time our portfolio was still worth about $20 million. We decided to go low risk and borrow $1 million against it, and put it into UrbanFetch. I figured we wouldn't do as well as a lot of other people were making out, but damn it, we were going to make a dime on the side.

At the time, UrbanFetch had just closed another round of $60 million financing. Our timing looked good. Then, a couple weeks after we closed the investment, the market tanked. The market started tanking like no one had ever seen before; all Internet stocks went down 90 percent. All the pre-IPO companies canceled their IPOs, and they all ran out of money. Kozmo burned through $250 million in under a year. And my own personal investment tragedy? Over eight months, I watched as the only cash I had left, the money I put into UrbanFetch, evaporated. I have nothing to show for it but a Rubik's Cube with their logo on it.

Individual trading is rarely nothing more than gambling, which is why I have no pity for those traders out there who lost money and blamed Todd and me. Hey, I lost a million dollars, but I'm not blaming UrbanFetch. I blame random variables and myself for investing at the wrong time. The market crapped out. That's it. Besides, I probably shouldn't have invested in the first place.

> > >

The month we stepped aside, Jenn and I took off on my first non-family vacation in a long while. We went to Venice via Florence and then ended up driving through Tuscan farmlands. Something about Italy, along with the fact that Chuck had just come on board, allowed me to ease off completely. There I was sitting in the Italian countryside with my girlfriend, listening to roosters, eating real northern Italian food, watching the sunset, then later, chilling on the beach in Elba. Paradise.

Then we came back to New York, and it hit me like a ton of massive scaffolding—my whole career had evaporated. My income was going to cease, and my worth, which rocketed from absolute zero to $97 million, had now dropped down to. . . . Well, our stock was now mired at $2 a share. I'd seen my net worth drop and drop and drop, and though I was technically still worth a few million bucks, it was all tied up in stock. I didn't have access to it, and I couldn't sell.

Why couldn't I sell? First, I would have inside information. Second, if a CEO or a board member sells and someone notices, it can cause a panic. There are so many restrictions, restrictions, restrictions; many of which were the reason why I could never liquidate anything before. It suddenly dawned on me that I might get nothing out of this, not a penny. For all intents and purposes, I was broke. I'd never really had cash in the bank. Now, I no longer had an income. But of course, everyone still perceived me as a billionaire.

Todd and I had a severance package that gave us enough cash for maybe a year. But the reality was that I had to figure something new out. Fast. But what? I was absolutely miserable. On top of that, my dad was still fighting to stay alive. He'd thus far been surviving terminal cancer, even as his own investment in TGLO was getting killed.

I needed to figure out what I was going to do with myself and how to make money again. At 26, I was having a midlife crisis.

That's when it happened with me and Jenn. Confronted with the abyss, I stepped away from her, and our relationship ended just like that. I wish I could take it all back. I was a fool. But I realize now that it had to happen so I could step away from everything and start again.

> > >

That August, the only thing that sustained me was this vague sense that there was something new I could go after, a new dream, and that this time around, I would do it better. From then on, I went into the office only on a part-time basis. I started reading fiction again for the first time in a long while.

I picked up the entire volume of *Dune*. I would go over to a jazz coffee bar on Seventeenth and Broadway and sit on a sofa in the back. As I delved into books, I was exploring space all over again and the prospect excited me.

It made me think of when Todd and I were initially excavating the Internet and of the time when I didn't spend my days and nights thinking about a damn stock price. Reading also took my mind off the terrible situation with Jenn. It took my mind off the situation with my dad, and it helped me jump-start my mind again, reviving my long-starved imagination.

It dawned on me that what I'd always liked the most about theglobe.com was the creative aspect, the making of something out of thin air, something that hadn't heretofore existed. I wanted to know how I could recapture that inspiration and what type of career would bring some of those elements back to me. One of the things I started doing after we stepped aside was taking notes. I started jotting down some of the feelings that came with the initial Net euphoria, and before I knew it, I was writing my memories. Little did I know they would ever wind up in a book.

I tried to simply tell the story of theglobe.com as it progressed, the same story I'd recapped so many times for my friends, only to find them listening in a state of excitement.

I thought maybe I could capture some of the elements that represented the Internet era and document this strange time in business history. I wanted to explain how it felt to be a religious crusader—back before money was to be made—so that there could be something dedicated to all those people who *did* take the risk of committing to a completely new world. A world that was totally uncharted at the time.

> > >

A few months after we'd stepped aside, I had to fly out to Los Angeles to wrap up some business. On the way back (it must have been the airplane food), I found that I needed to use the bathroom. As I was waiting at the cabin in the back, this guy who was sitting in the back row said, "Hey, I just wanted to let you know that I think what you did is amazing."

So I awkwardly said, "Um, who do you think I am?" He said, "You're Steph Paternot, the guy from theglobe.com."

His name was Brad Fuller, a film producer in Los Angeles. Had I ever thought of telling my story as a movie? Ironically, I'd just made the momentous decision that very weekend that I wanted to channel my creative drive into film. It was too bizarre. Ever since the launch of theglobe.com, my life had been filled with these strange moments of serendipity, where planets align and a little coincidental meeting led to something great.

Now here's some L.A. guy who thinks I'm story worthy. He brought up the *Rocky* story as an analogy to our experience. And it was—at least in the sense that Rocky loses his match in the end but still comes out a winner.

"Success," Brad said, "has to do with what you *did*, what you *achieved*." I liked the sound of that. So Brad and I arranged to meet and started to build a rapport. As of today, we've got a dozen projects in the works, and I'm fully ready to embark on a journey in the arts: writing, producing films, even acting. In the fall of 2000, I teamed up with Jannu Goldschmidt, a graduate of NYU Film School, and he directed my first short film called "Shutter." As of this writing, the film has been a finalist in four international festivals.

Now, as I'm about to take on a career in a new industry, it reminds me of the time when Todd and I started theglobe.com with absolutely no one, no friends, no girlfriends, no allies, no nothing. What I *do* have this time around is the experience I gained and the confidence of knowing that I can go from the depths of emotional despair and fight my way back up again.

And that's exactly the journey I'm ready for. Now, when I lie around at night and think, I put on trance music and get that same rush I would feel at Cornell. It *is* going to happen, and this *is* going to be a far more exciting ride. I can absolutely feel that this is my calling.

What role I'll play in the overall shaping of my next career I don't know, but I'm going to build it up from nothing. And I'll have much more longevity than the entrepreneur who starts as a creative person and has to eventually relinquish his baby to another CEO. After theglobe.com, I never want to be in another position where I build an asset only to have it taken away.

I want to *be* the asset.

> > >

When we stepped aside in January, we were cremated again by the press. All the usual suspects bared their fangs, but then the press had to widen their lenses.

WebVan went from a $25 stock down to 7 cents; Pets.com and their loveable sock puppet shut the entire company down. Drugstore.com tanked. Even Jeff Bezos and Tim Koogle saw their babies go way, way down.

VA Linux may be the classic example of injustice in the press. They performed far worse from a stock perspective than theglobe.com, yet they never faced the level of negativity that we enjoyed.

Though they had taken over our spot as the fastest-rising IPO in history, there was virtually no coverage about their failure from a stock market perspective. There's a sweet irony: Right after they went public, their CEO, Larry Augustin, was interviewed in some industry magazine. Inevitably, the reporter brought up the comparison to theglobe.com. His response was, "Oh, I would never want to be like theglobe.com. That would be bad."

Well, I'm pleased to say that they weren't like theglobe.com. Whereas it took us 1.5 years to drop 90 percent in value, it took them only 6 months.

> > >

Were we doomed to failure?

Maybe not. For Todd and me, there was a strange satisfaction in the dog days of 2000.

As early as 1995, people had always questioned how Internet companies would make money. Everyone said an advertising-based model was outlandish—it couldn't work. I can't tell you how many people told me that.

What I would try to point out is that this model has worked for years with network television, magazines, and newspapers. You built up an audience, you refined the demographics, you sold advertising space. When you had the right critical mass in each of those components, you became viable.

But people just couldn't get that through their heads. "Advertising can't work," was the mantra, "you've got to chase after e-commerce."

And then it was all about browsers, then all about push technology. "No, no, it's about Java. No, no, no, okay, hold on—it's all about Linux." There were always waves, there were microwaves within these waves, and the press and investors chased like lemmings after the next swell.

My point is that the only profitable and near-profitable Internet models that have worked to date—Yahoo, CNET, Lycos, Double-click—are all advertising players. And, yes, Amazon will ultimately work (hopefully) and Ebay works extremely well. But by far and large, the advertising concept works.

Now consider theglobe.com. Oh, but theglobe.com is a community.

Community can't work—that's what everyone says. But you know what? Community is just another function of what your audience is doing, as is playing in our games network. Our business is entirely about capturing an audience and getting them to do something. Think of Yahoo as *Friends,* and theglobe.com as *Seinfeld.* You can't say, "Oh, I understand the *Friends* business model. But the *Seinfeld* one is completely different." It's the same thing, only the scale is different.

The reality is that I have always believed theglobe.com can work. I believe today that it's just a question of raising enough money and getting to the breakeven point, and—for God's sake—staying up until it can get to that point.

But we were barraged with criticism, and our stock went down and down. We were always the sore thumb. And that became a death sentence. I think it was ridiculous. It still is. Vindication came when NASDAQ crapped out and the Internet got hammered. It became obvious that EToys hadn't made it and WebVan had plummeted. Healtheon and Go.com had come down. Disney took a $900 million write-off.

It wasn't just us. No longer were we the only idiots in town. From the biggest players to the littlest, from the most experienced CEOs to the least practiced, everyone was shaken up. We were no better and no worse than any of those top players.

Now, if you ask most experts where the Net is going and what's going to make it, most people cite the model I just described. Internet usage is *not* going down, it *has* revolutionized people's lives, and it *will* continue to grow. Advertising on the Net is rising; the quality of services for those companies that stay in business is growing as well.

We can't turn back. Who can imagine a day without the Net? Without e-mail? The Web is here to stay no matter what. Remember, there was a gold rush in California; but when the gold went away, California remained. It has transformed us. And the Net is continuing. Many of the best players have no intention of giving up. I believe theglobe.com can continue. I am a huge believer, and that is why I still own stock—even though I could sell it now. I still hold most of it because I believe in it.

EPILOGUE

People often ask me if I regretted actually going public or if there could have been another way to do it.

The answer, of course, is yes and no. With hindsight, I would have much preferred staying private because life then doesn't become determined by a stock price or the valuation of the company. Anyone who wants to get into it does so because of a belief in the business, not necessarily to make a quick buck.

In *Losing my Virginity* by Richard Branson (one of my and Todd's greatest idols), the great Brit entrepreneur talks about how unhappy he was after going public. Now Virgin is private again. I really would have loved the chance to take theglobe.com private again. But the reality is that I'm glad we went public.

I'm glad for the experience, and I'm glad because back then it was a necessity, a rite of passage. After all, going public gives you credibility and lets you grow your business faster; it attracts the advertisers and the investors. And you get cheap capital.

In the final analysis, it was a necessity. It had to be done.

From a personal stance, I sometimes wish I could take it back.

But . . . *whatever.*

No matter what happens, all I know is that we had a great idea. I believe there will always be hot new concepts that appear online, like a Napster. When the mania surrounding Napster dies off, a new thing will pop up. Today, it's cycled forward into an Internet *evolution,* and it will evolve, one step at a time, year after year. Still, I do honestly think the hype will never be so intense. I was there for the Internet *revolution.*

APPENDIX

where are they now?

Ed resigned from Mike's troop shortly after we did and joined Prime Ventures in Los Angeles. He also briefly became president of Dr. Koop. We still remain great friends.

Mike took over some of his old job managing Alamo as part of a new AutoNation spin-off. He's also still chairman of theglobe.com, and Todd and I continue to enjoy hanging out with him whenever he's in town.

All our covering analysts and most others in the industry for that matter quit or got fired, and some even joined Net companies that got downgraded by their peers.

Shortly after Todd and I resigned, Will and Bryan themselves left to join Net2Phone, another victim of the Internet bubble.

Todd is contemplating doing an MBA, after which he might move to Italy with his girlfriend.

My dad is in better health, and I hope we'll be even closer after he reads this book.

Last, and most important to me, my mom is still living in London, more energetic than I've ever seen her. Having raised and supported all of us through good times and bad, she shows no signs of slowing. I could not have made it through the last few years without her help, and I'll always have the comfort of knowing that when I steer my ship into port for repairs, she'll be there.

For more information on Steph's adventures visit www.paternot.com or send e-mail to averypublicoffering@paternot.com.

CAST

Stephan Paternot   Founder & CEO of theglobe.com

Todd Krizelman   Founder & CEO of theglobe.com

Michael Egan   Chairman of theglobe.com

Ed Cespedes   Head of M&A and Egan's chief financial expert

Ace Greenberg   Chairman of Bear Stearns

Yves Paternot   Steph's Father

James Cramer   Editor at Thestreet.com

Steve Frank   Wall Street Journal Reporter on CNBC

Bob Halperin   TGLO board member

David Horowitz   TGLO board member

Wayne Huizenga   TGLO board member

Mary Meeker   Analyst at Morgan Stanley

Vinod Khosla   Partner at Kleiner

David Wetherell   Chairman of CMGI

Larry_Hey   Anonymous poster in message boards

Alan Greenspan   Chief Economist for US Government

Bob Wright   President of NBC

Charlie Rose   Charlie Rose

David Filo   Founder of Yahoo

Henry Blodget   Merrill Lynch Analyst

Hunter Rawlings   President of Cornell

Jan Hopkins   CNN anchor

Jason McCabe Calacanis   Editor&Chief at Silicon Alley Reporter

Jeff Bezos   CEO of Amazon

Jerry Yang   Founder of Yahoo

Jonathan Weber   Editor&Chief at Industry Standard

Laurent Massa   CEO of Xoom

Lou Dobbs   CNNfn President

Mia Bergendahl   Steph's Mother

Index

233